AMERICAN HERITAGE SERIES

AMERICAN HERITAGE SERIES (Cont'd)

With Sword and Pen

The Adventures of
Captain John Smith

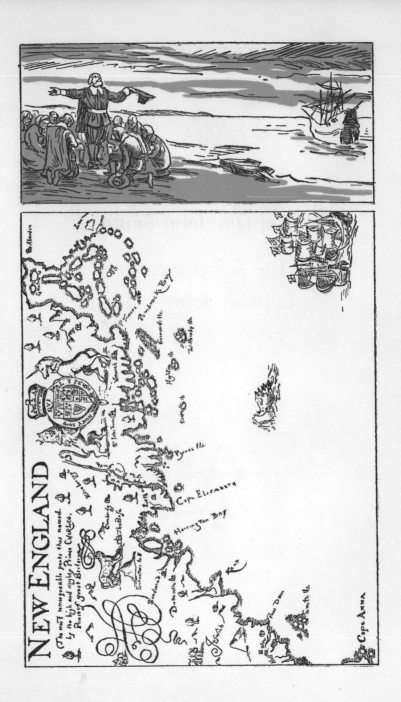

NEW ENGLAND

The most remarqueable parts thus named.
by the high and mighty Prince CHARLES,
Prince of great Britaine.

Cape ANNA

Smith Ils.

Harrington Bay

Cape ELIZABETH

Pymes Ils.

St John Town

Norwich

Penbrock Bay

With Sword and Pen

(The Adventures of) Captain John Smith

by Bradford Smith

Illustrated by David Hunt

ALADDIN BOOKS

New York: 1956

LIBRARY OF CONGRESS CATALOG CARD NUMBER: 56-5196

ALADDIN BOOKS IS A DIVISION OF AMERICAN BOOK COMPANY

PRINTED IN THE UNITED STATES OF AMERICA

Contents

After three hundred and fifty years, there are naturally many details about the life of John Smith which cannot be known. Some of these have been filled in to complete the narrative. But all the people and the main events are presented in this story as accurately as more than two years of research and the discovery of hitherto unknown documents could make them. The full story is given in *Captain John Smith: His Life and Legend.*

John Smith Sees the Wide World

☙ IT WAS ALREADY LIGHT WHEN John Smith woke up on a spring morning in 1590. The minute he woke up, the boy knew there was something exciting about the day. But what was it? He was still too sleepy to know that.

He lay on his back, looking up at the low ceiling where the shadows of new leaves were gently nodding. Soon he would know what was so very special about today. But it was almost as much fun wondering as it was to know. It was just like waiting for a surprise.

Suddenly he sat up. Now he knew! Today

was the beginning of Easter vacation. For thirteen days he could do just as he liked. It wasn't as much as at Christmas, when they had fifteen days. However, since these were the only vacations in the whole year, every day was precious. He mustn't waste a minute of it in bed. Ten years old, John was full of plans for every day of the school holiday.

"Francis! Wake up!" John began to shake his brother by the shoulder. Francis slept in the same big bed with him. He was only a year younger than John, and they were always together; John was the leader. It was he who always thought up their games and planned their adventures.

Francis didn't wake up easily. John shook his brother again and called, "Francis! It's Easter holidays! Wake up! It may be Mr. Sadler will take us up in the church tower today."

For months, John had ached to climb the narrow stone stairs up to the very top of the church tower. The church was in the heart of Willoughby—scarcely more than a stone's throw from the Smith farm if you cut across the fields. Its stone tower was always in sight even when the roofs of the village houses and the sturdy gray stone roof of the church itself were hidden by leafy tree branches.

The bell tower could be reached only by stairs guarded by a heavy oaken door to which Mr. Sadler, the parson, kept the key. John had often begged to explore the tower, to see the view from its height.

"It's too cold today, lad," Mr. Sadler would say. Or, "The clouds are so thick, you'd not be able to see a thing." At last, he had said, "Perhaps at Eastertime."

John jumped out of bed. He put on his long hose and breeches and tied them at the knee. He put on his doublet, which also took the place of a shirt. Then he remembered that he hadn't said his prayers.

He knelt beside the bed. It was a very short prayer. "Please God, bless us all and let Mr. Sadler take me up into the tower this day. Amen."

He tickled Francis until his brother crawled out of bed. While Francis was dressing, John made the bed. Then together they clattered down the stairs into the kitchen. His mother was there, but his father had already gone out to the fields. A farmer had more than he could do when spring came around.

John poured some water into a basin, washed his hands, and smoothed down his hair. If it had been a school day he would have brushed his cap and cleaned his shoes. But today he could hardly wait to get outside. Through the open door came the sweet smell of apple blossoms on a shaft of warm sunshine. Instead of being shut up in a schoolroom, he could be out there all day.

He ran to the door.

"We're going over to the church," he told his mother. "Come on, Francis."

"It's planting time," Mrs. Smith said. "Your father needs your help."

John felt as if a cloud had suddenly hidden the warm spring sun. But he knew that the church tower would have to wait.

He and Francis found their father in a field behind the house. He was plowing with his sturdy pair of oxen, but stopped when he saw the boys.

"Hallo there, you sleepyheads," he called. "Have you come to fetch me in to dinner?"

John grinned. It was not yet seven o'clock in the morning. His father was always joking.

"No, sir," John said. "We came to tell you that you were too late for it."

George Smith threw back his head and laughed. It made John happy to see his father with his head thrown back in the sun, laughing so that his shoulders shook.

George Smith was a farmer because his father had been a farmer before him. In England, in 1590, a man expected to be what his father had been. But George Smith loved horses more than he loved farming. He had a stable full of them, to ride and to train. Even Lord Willoughby came to Farmer Smith for horses.

Lord Willoughby was the one who owned a great part of the land in this section of England. George Smith's house was his to live in, the fields were his to work, to rent out, to leave to his sons, only by the permission of his lordship. Under the feudal system which had held sway in England for as long as people could remember, a farmer like John's father could never own his land outright. As soon expect the sun to shine at night!

"Well," said George Smith, his laughter gone, "you're not too late to plant beans. You'll find them in the larder. Mind you set a straight row."

The boys ran back to the house and returned with the leather bucket in which the

planting beans had been stored last fall.
When they had planted the long rows it
would be all right to go over to the church.
Their father had not mentioned any other
chores.

The sun was high when John and his
brother were finished. Would Mr. Sadler be
at the church now?

"Come on!" John called. With Francis at
his heels, he started at a run, down the winding lane which led to the gray stone church.

The boys ran around to the porch, stepped
up onto the big stone threshold and peered
in through the open door. There was no one
in sight.

If they sat down in a pew and perhaps
prayed a little—would he come? After a long
wait John heard a noise in the room beside
the altar. In a moment, he saw the parson
come out. John stood up in the aisle.

"Good morning, sir," he said. "It's a fine
morning, isn't it?"

Mr. Sadler squinted in the dim light of the
church. He rested his hands on his round
stomach. "Oh, it's you, John Smith," he said.
"What brings you into church on a fine morning like this?"

"We thought — that is, Francis and I —

maybe you'd take us up in the tower." John's heart beat fast.

Mr. Sadler looked down at his stomach and sighed. "Well —" he began. But this time he couldn't think of any excuse.

John had already run down the aisle to stand at the little door which led into the tower. Mr. Sadler opened it and started up. The dark, spiral stairs were so narrow, John wondered whether the parson would get stuck.

It seemed a long time before a gleam of sunlight appeared above them, but at last they came out on the level where the bells were.

"Here we are, then," puffed Mr. Sadler.

A big window was cut on each side of the belfry to let out the sound of the ringing bells. But the openings had wide slats so the boys could see hardly anything at all. John caught sight of more winding stairs.

"Can't we go to the top?" he asked. "You can wait here for us if you'd rather not climb any more," he said. Without waiting for permission, he started up to the tower roof.

The sun was brighter than ever after the long, dark climb, and the smell of apple blossoms floated even to this great height. Carefully he leaned over the stone wall and looked down. There was his own house with its big square chimney. And there was his father out in the field with the oxen. Everything looked small, yet very sharp and clean under the bright sun.

He ran to another side and there was the village of Alford, three miles away, where he went to school. He could see the tower of St. Wilfrid's Church and even the window of the room over the porch where school was held.

Now to the east!

"Look, Francis! It's the sea!" he shouted.

The boys leaned against the stones and squinted at the smooth, glassy surface of the English Channel shining in the sun.

John sighed. The sea was a road that led everywhere. It led to Holland, where Lord Willoughby had gained glory helping the Dutch fight the Spanish. It led to Italy and Turkey—even to far places like Africa and America. Would he ever see these places with his own eyes?

No, he was a farmer's son. That meant he would be a farmer, too. But he could dream. He tried to guess what it would feel like to stand at the bow of a ship with the wind and the spray beating against his face. What a wonderful life that would be, to sail across the ocean . . .

"John, look! Come here, quick!" Francis was calling from the other side of the tower. He was jumping up and down and pointing. "The pigs are loose. They're in the sown fields!"

John made for the stairs. Last year his father had been fined for letting his pigs get into the fields of barley and beans. He stumbled down the steep spiral stairs and out into the sunlight, passing the puzzled parson on the way. Anxiously, the two boys ran crosslots toward the field where the pigs were.

"The pigs are loose!" they shouted. Their father heard them and came running. John darted toward the fattest pig. The pig grunted and ran.

Francis reached for a young pig. Frightened, the animal swerved and ran right between Francis' legs. Squealing and squirming, the pig carried the boy along on its back.

Now Mrs. Smith came running from the house, shouting and waving her apron. The pigs squealed and ran everywhere except where the Smiths wanted them to go.

At last, when everyone was exhausted, the old sow went grunting back toward the farmyard with the other pigs following. The Smiths formed a circle behind them, to make

sure they wouldn't turn back. Then George Smith and his two sons mended the fence so that the animals wouldn't get out again.

"If I had my choice," he grumbled, "I'd take horses and let others have the pigs."

"Aye," his wife answered, "but I notice you eat your share of ham and bacon. The pigs be a nuisance for sure. But a farm's not a farm without them."

George Smith did not bother to answer. "Speaking of horses," he said to his sons, "I've promised to take the two-year-old colt to Lord Willoughby. Either of you boys want to come along?"

"I do!" John shouted. To go to Grimsthorpe! It was fifty miles away. John had never been so far in his life.

"Well, if we get our planting done, we'll go next week."

For the rest of the week John worked as hard as a man. His father had told him many times about the great manor house at Grimsthorpe where Lord Willoughby lived with his family and a house full of servants. Now he would see it for himself, and perhaps even see the great lord under whom they held their land—through whose pleasure they prospered or starved.

"Faster," John urged if he saw his younger brother lagging. "You heard Father say if the planting gets done we'll ride to Grimsthorpe!"

Lord Willoughby's Son
Makes a Promise

☞ "THERE IT IS!" SAID GEORGE SMITH. He reined in his horse and pointed ahead of him up the slope. At the top of the hill stood Grimsthorpe. It was the biggest house John had ever seen. At each end stood great, square stone towers. Between them stretched a long building with a dozen chimneys, eight pointed gables and more windows than he could easily count. Vines grew part way up the gray stone walls but stopped before they got to the third story, which was built into the roof. Huge as it was, the great manor house had a friendly look.

"We must ride round to the gate," his father said. "His lordship will see that we get a bite of supper, no doubt. Poor lads, you must be starved and tired, too."

They had started off shortly after dawn, and only stopped to eat some bread and cheese beside the road.

Yes, John thought, I guess I'm tired—a little. But he wouldn't have admitted it to anybody. He loved to ride a horse. His father had taught him almost before he could walk, and he rode to school every day. But fifty miles—that was the longest ride he had ever taken.

He was riding the colt that was to be left with Lord Willoughby. On his way home he would ride Dick, the horse he called his own, and take Francis up behind him.

The road dipped around a curve and the gables and chimneys of Grimsthorpe disappeared from view. Then, at the top of the gentle slope, they came to a gate guarded by a keeper.

George Smith explained their errand to the gatekeeper and the gates swung open. The three travelers trotted, side by side, into a big yard in front of the stables.

When John climbed down off his horse, his

legs were so stiff he could hardly stand. However, he forgot about his stiffness when a man with two boys strode from the big house toward the stables.

George Smith jerked off his hat and began to bow. "Good evening, your Lordship," he said. "I've brought the two-year-old you were pleased to have me raise for you." He stroked the nose of the horse John had ridden. "She's a beauty, Milord, if I do say it myself. Plenty of spirit, too. A bit skittish still but well broken to the saddle."

John kept a light hand on the reins but his eyes were fastened on Lord Willoughby, who had just come back from the wars in France. Queen Elizabeth herself had sent the great man to the war. The boy studied the pointed, black beard and narrow, thoughtful face. His quick gaze took in the clothes made of rich-looking velvet and silk and the thick gold chain hung around his lordship's neck.

He was already daring to dream of having garments like that himself someday, when he felt someone poking him in the ribs.

"I say, *can't* you hear? I asked you what your name is?"

He looked around, and there was the older of the two handsomely dressed boys who had come to the stables with Lord Willoughby.

"John Smith," John stammered. He wasn't quite sure whether he had to call this boy "Milord" or not. The boy seemed younger than himself, so he decided not to. "That's my brother Francis," he added, gaining confidence.

"I'm Robert Bertie, and that's my brother, Peregrine. He's named after my father, but I'm a year older."

John remembered that noble families always had several names. Lord Willoughby's full name was Peregrine Bertie, Lord Willoughby d'Eresby.

"Can you ride?" Robert Bertie continued.

"I rode the colt down here from Willoughby," John answered. "It took us all day."

Lord Willoughby had finished examining the two-year-old. Now he asked George Smith to come into the stables and look over some of his other animals.

The men had scarcely disappeared before Robert had hoisted himself up onto the back of the colt. John felt the loosely held reins jerked out of his hand. He saw the frightened animal give a start, then bolt toward the gate.

Francis and young Peregrine went running with cries of alarm into the stables. John leaped onto his father's mare and followed Robert through the gate.

The colt had a head start and he was scared. John leaned forward on his horse and brought his feet up so as to hold onto her belly. He prodded with his toe. "Come on, lady," he called, leaning close to the mare's ear. "We've got to catch up. Come on!"

They clattered down the hill, around the wide curve, and out onto a straight piece. John could see that Robert was having a hard time to stay on the colt. If he slipped off, he would be badly hurt—perhaps killed.

"Hug with your legs!" John shouted. "Grab his mane!"

Robert was riding one of the fastest beasts George Smith had ever raised. John wondered if he could ever overtake him.

He kept encouraging the mare and little by little he caught up. At last he rode neck and neck with Robert's horse.

"Whoa now," he called, "whoa!" He reached out and seized the bridle. Both steeds slowed down. Then they stopped and stood quietly side by side.

Now Lord Willoughby and George Smith came galloping down the hill. Behind them were several stable men.

"Are you all right, Robert?" Lord Willoughby asked. "Never jump on a strange horse, my boy. Make sure he knows you first." Then he turned to John. "That was good riding, lad," he said. "I see you've learned of a good teacher. I'll not forget what you've done."

Now the whole party turned and rode back up the hill.

"Come in and have supper," Lord Willoughby said after they had left the horses at the stable. "Then we'll see that there are beds for you. You must be tired after so long a ride."

"I want that boy to sleep in my room," Robert declared, pointing at John.

After brushing the dust off their clothes and washing in the kitchen, the Smiths were led into the great hall. There, at one end of a long table sat Lord Willoughby and his lady, the two boys, several other children and officers of the big household whose duties John could only guess at. The Smiths took their places near the middle of the table, between the officers and the servants of the household. Then at a signal from his lordship everyone stood up.

"Master Johnston will please to say grace," said Lord Willoughby, fixing the young man next to John with his eye.

After the "Amen," there began such a passing of dishes as John had never seen before. Cold roasts of meat, bread and cheese, pitchers of wine, vegetables and meat pies and puddings—all came marching from hand to hand around the table until it seemed that there was hardly time to eat anything.

When the meal ended, grace was said again. Then Robert and Peregrine came to lead John and his brother on a tour of the house. They visited the chapel with its carved altar and climbed the stairs to the gallery overlooking the great hall. They went up into one of the big square towers and out onto the roof. Since Grimsthorpe was built on a hill, John could see even farther than he had from Willoughby church. And again, as he looked, he felt that ache inside him to travel to far places.

"I'm going to cross the ocean when I grow up," he said.

"How are you going to get there?" said Robert. Plainly, he thought the farmer's son was boasting.

"I — I don't know. But I'll get there somehow."

"I'll have my father send you with me," Robert said, carelessly. "I'm going when I'm older. To France. Father said I should."

From the roof they went down many stairs into a room below ground. Robert called it the dungeon.

"Do you ever put people in here?" Francis asked.

"We would if they were bad. I guess we don't have any bad people around Grimsthorpe," Robert added, with part of a sigh.

When they came up into the great hall again, the man who had said grace at supper was waiting for them.

"Time for bed, young masters," he said. Master Johnston must be their tutor, John thought. His father had told him that the boys had a private teacher to look after them.

"Can he sleep in my room?" Robert said, pointing again at John.

Peregrine echoed, "Francis is going to sleep in my room."

Master Johnston looked doubtful. These boys in homespun doublets were only the sons of a farmer.

"He's going to be my valet and go to France with me," Robert said.

This explanation seemed to satisfy Master Johnston. It showed that Robert had not forgotten his place in the world.

John was happy, too. He wasn't sure what a valet was, but since it meant that he would go to France with Robert, he didn't much care.

The next morning, when the Smiths started for home, John got up his courage to ask, "How am I going to know when you're ready to start for France?"

"I'll write you a letter," Robert said. "Can you read?"

There were many grown men who couldn't read, so John didn't object to the question.

"Yes, I can read," he said.

After they had said good-by and started up the road, he wished he had asked Robert not to wait until time to sail the ocean but to write him a letter soon. All the way home he thought about Lord Willoughby's son and the brave adventures they would have together in far places.

John Explores the Past

A YEAR WENT BY AND NO WORD came from the son of Lord Willoughby. John said nothing about Robert's promise but he was bitterly disappointed as the winter gave way to spring with no sign of a message summoning him to Grimsthorpe.

"It's time you went to a bigger school," Mr. Smith told his son. "King Edward's School in Louth is a fine place. Besides, I've business in the town. I can see you often."

Louth was sixteen miles away, too far to ride back and forth every day, so John would be living at the school. To a boy raised in the little village of Willoughby, Louth seemed big and exciting. He and his father rode into a large open space that was filled with people and animals. It was the Saturday market.

"Louth has two weekly markets, on Wednesday and Saturday. Farmers be coming from all over to sell their animals, their eggs and cheese," George Smith explained.

Geese cackled, cocks crowed, pigs grunted and cattle lowed. Men who had things to sell shouted to attract attention. The warm, lively, animal smell hung over the market. John wanted to stay and look at everything, but his father had no time to loiter. He had to deliver his son to the school and get back to Willoughby.

So they trotted through the market place without stopping and on past Saint James's church with its gray stone walls. A little farther on, near the Westgate, they turned left up a little hill.

"There's the school," said Mr. Smith.

John saw a building with walls of clay and timber, covered with a heavy-looking thatched roof. A few moments later he was inside the dark hall, shaking hands with the schoolmaster. Then his father said good-by and rode off, taking John's own horse, Dick, along.

John wished he could have kept his horse. They had always been good friends. He could talk to Dick the way he could never talk to people, not even to his brother Francis. On horseback, he felt that he was halfway toward the life of adventure he longed for. The excitement he had felt at coming away to school faded as he watched his father ride off. There seemed little chance for adventure in a crowded schoolroom.

Whenever he could get away from school for a few minutes, he ran down to the blacksmith's near the market. There, with the smell of burnt hoof and old harness and the hissing of red-hot horseshoes as they were thrust into the trough, he felt at home. He patted the horses, listened to the talk of the men and learned all they knew about the shoeing of the animals.

There was much to learn in Louth that was not in the schoolmaster's books. Just to walk down the street was a treat to a country boy with eyes as sharp as John's.

He liked to stop at the baker's to catch the sweet, heavy smell of newly baked bread pour out the door; to watch a cobbler at work making shoes. He made a habit of looking in at the butcher's where long strings of sausage were being made. He saw the twisted, bloody rag at the door of a barber-surgeon and stood in the doorway while a customer held his arm over a basin to be bled.

Everywhere he looked, there was something to interest him. Everywhere, except in the schoolroom! To study Latin and then more Latin and after that more Latin was a bore. To copy long sentences into his commonplace book seemed a waste of time. When he was out seeing the wide world he'd have no use for such things. John could not help looking out the window or squirming in his seat. Often when the master called on him, he had lost the place on the page.

The master kept a stout rod for those who could not answer his questions. John came to know the feel of it very well.

On Sundays and special church days the whole school would march down to church. One Sunday, as the long service went on and on, John grew more and more restless. He felt hemmed in by the boys sitting on both sides of him. He squirmed and pushed with his shoulders to get more room. The boys pushed back. Half in fun John and his schoolmates began an undercover war of pushes, thrusts and pinches.

The game started off gently enough. But each push naturally was a little stronger than the next. Elbows dug into ribs. Fingers were squeezed, legs pinched. Soon John's whole row was swaying like a tree in a high wind.

Just as the parson was saying "Amen" to a prayer, the boy at John's right gave his leg a sharp pinch.

"Ow!" John shouted. Then quickly, hoping it would be taken for a response to the prayer, "—men!"

The Dog Whipper, paid to keep dogs out of the church and boys in order inside, came down the aisle. He glared at the whole row of boys, and brought his whip down on John's shoulders.

"Stop your carryings on," he hissed, "or I'll lock you in the crypt." The crypt was the church cellar. It was full of graves, and though the boys had never seen it, they thought of it as a horrible place.

* * *

A few days later, John was wandering through the market place when he saw a crowd of men. People often got together this way to listen to travelers from other parts of England and sometimes a sailor or a soldier would bring news from some distant part of the world.   Always curious, the boy walked over to see what was happening.

"Who is it?" he asked a man standing near.

"Sh!   It's Job Hortop.   Him as was made a slave by the Spaniards."

John crawled and squirmed until he was in the front row.

"So there I was in America without a ship or any way to get home," Job Hortop was saying.   "The Spaniards have got their grips on that part of the world.   I don't need to tell you there's no love lost between us and the Spaniards.   They caught me and made a slave of me.   Sent me back to Spain and chained me into one of their galleys.   I hope I never see an oar again as long as I live."

"How long were you gone?" someone asked.

"Twenty-three years away from England, it was.   Pray God I'll never have to leave her again."

"Is it true that America is so full of gold the Indians use it for all their common pots and dishes?   Can you pick chunks of it from the earth?"

"There's gold enough there to make the Spaniards rich as Midas.   But they'll not let us Englishmen get our hands on any of it if they can help it."

John wanted to ask Job Hortop all about America, but some men invited the traveler to go into a tavern with them, so the boy heard no more.

* * *

At Louth, John first discovered the stories about knights of a bygone age. There were many books of this kind. The teacher frowned on them, so of course the boys read them every chance they got. Each boy managed to own one or two, and by swapping them back and forth they had plenty to read, for the books were long and the time they could snatch from their studies was short.

John's favorite was Tom - a - Lincoln. Though the knight's adventures had taken place hundreds of years ago, they seemed near and very real to John. Here was a hero from his own country who was the son of the famous King Arthur and a great fighter. His first great adventure was a trip to Portugal. Next he had traveled to a mysterious land peopled only by women. Another time he jousted in a great tournament, clad in armor and riding a jet-black steed.

John found more excitement in reading of the glorious olden days than in the market at Louth—even when the Fairs were held,

with their bear-baiting and plays in the courtyard of the inn.

As he read about Tom-a-Lincoln, John knew that this was the life he wanted to live. He wanted to travel to far places. He wanted a band of soldiers who would look up to him as their leader. He wanted to ride out on a fine horse with a sword in his hand and the enemy running in fear of his strength. He wanted to come home and be honored for his great deeds.

Only how could he get to be that kind of man? Studying Latin grammar at Louth didn't appear to be any help at all.

* * *

A year—two years—slipped by at Louth. John made friends there, as he did everywhere. But he felt as if he were marking time instead of marching ahead. He wanted to be doing things. Travel, danger, adventure—these were the things for him.

He was thirteen now. When it seemed as if he could not stay in the schoolroom another day, Easter vacation came. His father came for him, bringing his horse.

Dick whinnied with joy to see him. John stroked his nose, his back. Then he jumped on and sat very straight as they passed through the streets of Louth. But the minute they were in the country, John leaned over and whispered into Dick's ear: "Come on, boy. Let's see how you can go." At the same time he kicked gently with his heel.

Dick acted as if this were what he had been waiting for. He stretched his long legs and seemed almost to be flying through the air.

John hunched forward. He held the reins up close to Dick's head, but he held them loosely. The wind whistled past his ears. The blossoming hedges swept past. The school at Louth was far behind him now. He had forgotten it. He was a knight riding to defend a beautiful and helpless lady from the fire-breathing dragon. He was Tom-a-Lincoln. . . .

When they reached Willoughby he had to slow down and be John Smith again. He turned in at the church and trotted down the lane to his own house. And there were his mother and Francis and his sister Alice all waiting for him.

He jumped down off his horse and walked into the big room with the fireplace where his mother did the cooking. This room was their kitchen, their dining room, their living room. The floor was covered with fresh rushes. The

air smelled of wood smoke and beefsteak pie.
It smelled liked home.

"It's good to have you here, John," said his
mother.

"It's good to *be* here," said John. "Have
we got any new foals?"

"That we have," his father answered.
"Two fine new foals, newly born. Come out
to the stables and see them."

Alice, seven now, shyly took her brother's
hand. Francis ran on ahead. John lifted his
sister up onto the fence. The two foals with
their shiny, brown coats and their thin legs
were frisking about the yard. They tossed
their heads and pranced and chased each
other. It lifted John's heart to watch them.
That was how he felt, too, because it was
spring and he was home on holiday.

"See the two-year-old over there?" said
his father. "I'm taking him to Tattershall
tomorrow. Would you like to go along?"

Tattershall Castle, the home of the Earl of
Lincoln! It was a regular castle, the very kind
that knights had used to ride out from.

Next morning, John and Francis and their
father set out for the castle. Francis rode the
earl's colt which he had helped to train. John
felt the way he supposed a man would feel

who had been locked up in a dungeon. He kept racing Dick ahead, then coming back to meet the others. The twenty-five-mile journey seemed nothing at all.

At last John called, "There it is!"

Rising out of the flat country ahead of them was a huge tower of red brick. Tattershall looked so exactly like the castles he had read about that John had the strange feeling that he had been here before.

"Look!" he called. "There's a moat! And a drawbridge!"

He waited for Francis and his father to catch up. Then the three of them clattered across the bridge. A uniformed guard stopped them.

"I've brought a horse for the earl's stables," George Smith explained.

"Take it to the tilt yard. The riding master's there. He'll tell you what to do next."

The boys followed their father through a gate and out onto another drawbridge across a second moat. The towers of the bridge loomed ahead, with the great chains which could raise the bridge in time of war.

The travelers passed through the bridge tower and out onto a great open space in front of the castle. Now John had some idea of how huge the castle was. It was four stories high, with towers at each of the four corners that rose another story above the main roof. He reined his horse to gaze at the castle, and would hardly have been surprised if Tom-a-Lincoln had come riding across the field. This was the real thing!

His father and Francis were already half-way across the field. John touched his horse and cantered after them. They crossed a bridge which led them to the tilt yard.

And there, as if they had stepped out of a book of knighthood, two mounted men rode at each other with swords raised. John drew rein and watched with wide eyes.

The men shouted as they neared each other. Then, just as he thought they would crash, they turned aside and rode in opposite directions. Now they were turning. Again they rode toward each other. This time the two swords clashed with a ringing sound of steel.

"Will they try to kill each other?" John asked his father.

Mr. Smith laughed. "No, it's only practice," he said. "That's Polaloga, the riding master, teaching one of the earl's sons the art of jousting."

The farmer and his two sons sat on their horses and watched while Polaloga went on with the lesson. He galloped down the field. Scarcely slowing down at all, he turned his horse and came galloping back again. Then he watched while the earl's son did the same.

Next, he made his horse move with an in-and-out motion. At the same time, he slashed with his sword first on one side and then on the other, as if he were fighting off an enemy.

He put his horse through sudden turns such as John had never seen before. Sometimes he would make the animal rear back on his hind legs. Then he would make him kick with his forelegs. He made the steed jump into the air with all four feet, and kick out his hind legs as he came down. He made him leap up with his forefeet in the air and then kick out his hind legs before touching the ground.

John had thought himself a good rider. Now he realized that there was a whole science of riding which he knew nothing about. He *must* learn it. But how did you ever train a horse to do all those things?

When the lesson was over, the earl's son rode away, glancing at the Smith horses but paying no attention to their riders.

Then Polaloga came. He had a nose which

seemed to have taken command of his face and he spoke with a thick Italian accent. But his dark brown eyes were alive and friendly.

"You bring me the two-year-old?" he asked. He stepped up to the horse Francis was riding, and ran his hands over the horse's legs and body. He felt each muscle, stroked the animal's mane and nose and looked into his eyes.

"Good horse," he said. "Come with me, we get money."

Into the big castle the boys trooped with Polaloga and their father. In a room with a vast fireplace, at the top of the stairs, the earl's steward came forward and dropped some pieces of gold into George Smith's hand. Before John had time to look around they were on the stairs again.

A few minutes later they were on the road to Willoughby. Francis rode behind John. John kept looking back until his father smiled and said, "Why don't you put Francis in front and you ride backwards?"

John laughed, but he continued to stare until the castle was out of sight. He spent the rest of his vacation trying to teach his horse the tricks he had seen.

A Farmer's Son

⊂Ε THE JOURNEY TO TATTERSHALL
gave John something to think about when he
got back to school. But it also made the study
of Latin seem less attractive than ever. He
had kept hoping that he would get a letter
from Robert Bertie. Then they would go off
to France together. However, it seemed as if
Robert had forgotten him.

Day after day he looked out the school
window. He saw the clean white clouds
sailing in their ocean of blue sky. Even
clouds were going somewhere, while he just
sat in the same place.

It was more than he could stand. When classes ended, he took his books and ran down to the market place. The Wednesday market was open. He sold the books, put the few coins in his pocket, bought some bread and cheese, and started out for Boston, thirty miles away.

Boston, he knew, was a busy port. Ships always had two or three boys in their crew. He was sure he could get a job.

Just to be outdoors with the open road ahead of him was so wonderful that he ran as much as he walked. The sun beat down on his head and shoulders. Little clouds of dust rose with each step he took. He was not afraid of what he had done—just excited.

When suppertime came, he stopped by a small stream. He kicked his shoes and stockings off to cool his feet and broke a big chunk of bread from his loaf. With the bread in one hand and cheese in the other, he took a bite first from one and then from the other. He dipped his face into the stream to drink and let the cool water wash over his face.

It was beginning to grow dark when he came to a crossroad. Straight ahead lay the road to Boston. But if he turned to the left, he could soon be home at Willoughby. He stood in the road a long time. Then he kept straight ahead.

He moved more slowly now and tried whistling to keep up his spirits. Somehow the fun seemed to have gone down with the sun. A chill breeze blew across the flat lands. He looked for a place to sleep but could find no sheltering tree. So he kept on walking. His feet began to sting, and the ache worked up his legs. Darkness came. He could no longer see the road, and had to feel his way with his toes.

At last he made his way to a clump of trees. He sat down and leaned back against the trunk of one of them. He was cold and his feet hurt and he was very sleepy.

When morning came, he ate the rest of his bread and cheese and started toward Boston again. But he moved more and more slowly. At last, he turned around and started running back toward the road to Willoughby.

* * *

When he walked into the house, his mother looked at him as if she had seen a ghost. Then she ran and wrapped him in her arms. He let his head rest on her shoulder for a minute while she stroked his hair.

"Are you sick, John?" she asked. "Is something wrong? Have they sent you home?"

He tried to tell her how it had felt to be shut up in school, with the birds singing outside and the clouds sailing past the window. He found that he couldn't say much but his mother seemed to understand. Then he went up to bed and when he came down at noon he knew his mother must have explained everything, because his father asked no questions.

"We'll see how you like farming," he said. "If that doesn't agree with you—well, then we'll see."

At first John was so happy to be out of the classroom that he enjoyed the farm. Even in the busy seasons he could always find some time to ride his horse.

But as time went on, the long hours of work with hoe and shovel and plow grew tiresome. He still dreamed of adventure, and in the little village of Willoughby nothing ever seemed to happen.

One night after supper—John was fifteen now—the family were sitting around the big fireplace. "Well, John," said Mr. Smith, "what do you think of farming by now?"

There was only the light of the fire in the room. His father's face was almost hidden in shadow where he sat on the long settle. Perhaps the darkness gave John the courage he needed.

"Maybe I'd like it when I'm older," he said. "But now—well, I'd like to be seeing the world."

"The farm will be yours when I'm gone," George Smith said. "You are the elder son."

"It will not be mine," John blurted out, "and it's not truly yours. It will always belong to Lord Willoughby. I might like farming on acres that I owned."

"What an idea!" his mother murmured in a shocked voice.

But her son continued bluntly. "There are places in the world—sailors say so that have traveled afar—where land belongs to no one. Wide stretches that have never been worked, fields big as the ocean. A traveler told me so one day at Louth. He'd been to Africa and to America."

John's father sighed. "I can see you'll not be happy with farming until you've seen some of the world. I've some business at King's Lynn with Thomas Sendall. He's the greatest merchant in all this part of the world—he's even been lord mayor of Lynn. Perhaps he'll take you as his apprentice. He has ships

going to Holland. It may be, he'll put you on
one of them. What do you say?"

John jumped off his stool so quickly that he
kicked it over. "When can we go?' he said.

Mr. Smith laughed. "Well, not this evening," he said. "Maybe, in two or three
days."

A few days later John and his father set out
for King's Lynn. They went first to Wain-
fleet where they found a light open sailboat
which would take them across the wide bay
along the coast, called "The Wash."

The distance was less than thirty miles but
this was John's first sea voyage. He ran all
over the boat, and asked questions of an old
sailor. But, best of all, he liked to stand at the
bow, feeling the deck rise and fall beneath
him while the spray dashed against his face.

It was over much too soon. The boat sailed
up the Ouse River and the church steeples of
King's Lynn came in view. Then the boat
began to pass the "fleets" or canals which cut
the town into islands. The canals were
crowded with small boats and ships. Goods
brought from Holland could go by canal all
the way to London. Lynn was an important
port.

Now the boat tied up beside a high-peaked,

brick warehouse. A few minutes later John and his father were in the counting house or office of Thomas Sendall.

Sendall wore clothes as rich as a lord's, and John noticed that his father bowed to him as if he were as important a gentleman as Lord Willoughby.

"Yes, I can use the boy," he said. "He may live in my house with the other apprentices."

"He hopes to get to sea for a bit, Your Honor," said George Smith.

"Well, we'll put him in the counting house first. Then, we'll see."

So John went to work for Thomas Sendall. At first he only swept out the office or ran errands. He liked running errands because it gave him a chance to visit the ships, the warehouses, the Town Hall. Soon, he knew every street and canal in the town. He loved to stop along the river front and talk with the sailors. He asked them all sorts of questions about the places where they had been, until he knew the names of all the important seaports.

Some of the sailors had been to America. England's enemy, Spain, had got hold of most of America, it seemed. Why shouldn't England have a share in it too? John thought of the miraculous land—the free land a man could call his own. A plain man, called John Smith. Why not? His heart beat wildly at the thought.

Days and weeks went by and Thomas Sendall never mentioned letting him go to sea. At last the boy got up courage enough to speak about it.

"A ship?" said Mr. Sendall. "You don't like the work here? It isn't good enough for you?"

"Yes, sir. I like it. Only I've a great love for ships and I thought . . ."

"Later," said Mr. Sendall. "We'll see to it later."

John waited a few months and asked again. The answer was the same. At last, when a year had gone by, he decided to find a place on a ship for himself and leave Mr. Sendall. But, just as he was ready to leave, a traveling tinsmith brought a letter to Mr. Sendall's warehouse. It was addressed to *Master John Smith* and came from his brother, Francis.

"Father is sick," it said. "Mother says you are to come home at once."

The message was dated March 30, 1596. It had been three days on the way.

Mr. Sendall loaned John a horse, and he set

out for home at once. It was a long day's
ride. He reached home late at night. Francis
met him at the door.

"Father died this day," he said

          *   *   *

As the elder son it was now John's duty to
stay at home and run the farm. All day long,
he worked in the fields or cared for the animals. At first he could see that his mother
was afraid he couldn't do the work. However,
she soon came to rely on him. When he
brought in a pail of milk or a fresh-killed
chicken, she would smile or lay a hand on his
shoulder. Her wordless thanks was better
than any pay.

When they sat at dinner, he at one end of
the table and she at the other with Alice and
Francis between, she would ask him what
work he planned next. That made him feel
like a man. He tried hard to be one.

So he was not prepared for what happened
next.

A Mr. Martin Johnson began to come to the
house. He had long talks with Mrs. Smith
after the children were in bed. Then, one
day, he drew John aside.

"Your mother and I are going to marry,"
he said. "It's too much for you to care for this

farm by yourself. You can all come to live with me at my house."

"Let Francis and Alice go if they want," John said. "I can take care of myself."

He had done his best to care for his mother. He had done well. If she wanted to go with this Mr. Johnson, let her go. Bitterness ate into his heart. He made himself believe that he had no parents now. He was free to go where he liked, do what he liked.

The next day he left home, walked to Boston, and found a ship bound for Holland. There were English soldiers aboard going to help the Dutch fight the Spanish invaders. John went up to the captain, Joseph Duxbury, and asked to be taken on as a soldier. He was seventeen now and though he was short, he was sturdy.

"What know you of soldiering?" the captain asked.

John had read everything about soldiering that he could lay his hands on. He soon satisfied the captain.

For two years he marched and fought with the English troops. But he had a great desire to see his family again, to show off the fine doublet and velvet cloak he had bought out of his army pay, to boast a little of his soldiering.

He took ship for England but when he arrived in Willoughby, his family was not at Martin Johnson's farm.

*   *   *

The neighbors said they had moved away to Boston. "You should have come home two days ago," they said. "Lord Willoughby sent a messenger for you."

"Lord Willoughby?" Had Robert Bertie remembered his promise after all?

John ran into the pasture of their old farm, rented, now, to strangers. Dick, his horse, knew him and came cantering up to him. Within a few minutes John had him saddled and was riding as hard as he could go, to Grimsthorpe.

When the great stone towers and the many chimneys of Grimsthorpe came in view, John urged his tired old horse up the hill and entered by the stable gate. He handed the reins to a stable boy, brushed some of the dust off his handsome new clothes and walked confidently down to the house.

"His Lordship sent for me," John said to the servant who answered the bell. "John Smith, of Willoughby."

While he waited in the great hall he looked at the portraits on the walls. There was one of Lord Willoughby himself, with pointed black beard which made his face look thin, thoughtful and rather sad.

"There you are!"

John whirled around. Young Peregrine was walking toward him. But when he saw John's brocaded doublet, velvet cloak and sword, he hesitated. "Are—are you John Smith?" he asked.

John looked down at his clothes. Then he laughed. "These are all I have to show for two years of fighting in Holland," he said. "John Smith, your father's tenant, at your service, Master Peregrine." He bowed with a fine flourish, for he was no longer a country boy but a soldier who had seen the world. "I believe your father sent for me."

"He wants you to go to France with my tutor and me. Robert's over there already. He's been there a year. We'll tour the whole country together."

They had not forgotten him after all!

Several days later, toward the end of June, the three riders set out on horseback for London and the English Channel. Robert was waiting for them at Orléans, so they took a ship to Le Havre and rode inland through Normandy, toward the Loire River.

Robert was as surprised as Peregrine had been to see what a change had taken place in John. Those years in Holland had made a man of him. At nineteen he had already faced death and learned that he had the courage to face it. It was not only the clothes that were new, but the person inside them.

Robert had expected a farm boy who would wait on him hand and foot, the son of a tenant farmer who would be happy to serve as a valet. Instead, he found a gentleman-soldier, not only older and more experienced but just as well dressed as himself. One might almost think that there was no difference between a lord and a commoner! At first Robert did not know how to act.

"Captain Smith," he called John jokingly, "I told you we'd tour France together. Now we will."

Peregrine and the tutor took their cue from Robert. Soon they had almost forgotten that John Smith was not their social equal.

For several months the four rode through France from one end to the other. In November they found themselves back at Orléans. Robert and Peregrine were to spend the winter in Paris but John decided to return to Willoughby. He had had enough of aimless traveling for a while. So they parted with no hint of how much was to happen to change the life of the young soldier before they met again.

John did not get back to England as quickly as he had planned. He went first to see some of his soldier friends in Holland and took ship from there. But the vessel was wrecked off the English Coast. He swam ashore, sick and weak, his fine clothes ruined.

The land at Willoughby was rented to another tenant, though since his mother had married John received the rent. John's father had also been allotted a piece of woodland, distant from any town. This piece was John's to use by Lord Willoughby's permission. There the young man went, on a fine horse his father had left him, and there he built himself a kind of tent made of boughs.

It was spring again—the spring of 1600. The trees were in flower; their sweet smell filled the air.

John had seen enough of warfare to know that he would make a good soldier. But he had also seen enough to know that he still had a great deal to learn. Mounted on his horse, he practiced for hours with his lance. He hung a ring from a tree and rode at it until he could run the lance through it at a fast charge. He exercised with his sword until his arm was almost as hard as the steel itself. When he grew tired, he lay on the bank of a stream and read a book called *The Art of War*.

This was the life he had dreamed of as a boy—the life of a warrior-knight. Knighthood was out of fashion in England, but he had heard that single combat was still practiced in Hungary, where a bitter war was going on. That was where he planned to go, as soon as he was ready.

But how would he know when he was ready?

Tattershall! He remembered the visit he had made there with his father, years ago. If the Italian riding master was still there, he would be able to judge. With some regret John left his hiding place in the woods and set out for Tattershall.

Adventure Comes High

◖❧ WHEN JOHN RODE UP TO THE
castle gate, his horse was combed and fur-
nished like the finest gentleman's. His clothes
would have become a lord.

"I want to learn all the arts of military
riding," he told Polaloga.

The riding master was delighted to have a
young man who wanted to learn and who
really planned to put his knowledge to use.
Day after day, he put John through all the
tricks of riding.

It was hard work. But John kept at it

because he knew his life might some day depend upon it.

When they began practicing with lances, the master often knocked John off his horse. For days at a time his body was covered with bruises. Then one day John charged down the field. He lowered his lance at just the right time. He made his horse swerve at the right moment. And Master Polaloga fell to the ground!

John ran to help him. He was sure the riding master would be angry. Instead of that, his face was spread with smiles. "Good, good!" he said in his strong Italian accent. "When you knock me off ten times, I let you go."

When John was not riding or tilting, he was fencing with some of the men in the earl's household. At last Polaloga was satisfied that the young soldier was ready for Hungary.

From King's Lynn, John sailed across to Holland where he met four Frenchmen. "Come with us to France," they said. "We'll introduce you to the Duchess of Mercoeur. Her husband is general of the armies fighting the Turk. She will give you a letter to him."

So John set sail with them for France. They reached their port at night. When

John's trunk was put into the small boat that would take them ashore, there was no room left for him. His friends promised to take care of the trunk and to send the boat back for him immediately. It did not return until the next day. By then John could find no trace of the Frenchmen nor of his trunk. All his money and his clothes were in it. He had to sell his cloak to pay for the voyage.

After wandering about in France, cold and hungry, John was finally helped by the Earl of Plouer, who gave him clothes and food and entertained him in his castle. With money in his pocket once again, John set out for Marseilles. There, he took ship for Italy.

But bad luck stuck close to John on this trip. Stormy weather forced the vessel to put into the harbor of Nice. Some of the passengers decided that the foreigner was bringing bad luck to the ship. Setting sail again, they threw him overboard. He managed to swim to a little island, and the next morning was taken off by a ship's captain who was a neighbor of the Earl of Plouer. At last, after a voyage into the Mediterranean, John was put ashore in Italy.

At Siena, John found his old friends, the Bertie brothers. When he told them of his plan to fight in Hungary, Robert shrugged his shoulders and said, "You've lands of your own at home. Why risk your neck in a war that has nothing to do with you?"

"I have no land. I have only the right to rent fields from his lordship, your father. In Lincolnshire I'm a tenant farmer," John said bluntly. "In Hungary I may become a captain of troops. And after that—who knows? You were born with all the honors you need. I must make mine."

"Then good luck to you, Captain," said Robert, with a trace of ridicule in his voice.

John Smith arrived in Hungary and made his way to the fighting front with all speed. The Hungarian officers were impressed with the bold young Englishman and the tricks of warfare he had learned.

He had not been in camp long before the Turks besieged the walled town of Oberlimbach. The soldiers inside the town were cut off. The commander of the main body of the army did not know how to get a message to the besieged troops.

John explained how a message could be sent into the town by the use of torches. Flaming torches spelled out a message: "We will charge to the east, Thursday night.

When we attack, you come out and join us."

Before the siege began, Smith had mention this method of signaling by torch to Herbertsdorf, who was now in command of the forces in the town.

John waited anxiously as the flaming torches spelled out the code. Would Herbertsdorf be able to read the signals? Would he understand?

When an answering signal from within the town rose in the air, John Smith's reputation was made.

At the time of the attack, John introduced another trick he had learned in Holland. He fastened pieces of fuse to long strings. One soldier at each end carried these strings onto the field. When they were lighted, it made the enemy think there were hundreds of troops with the fuses of their guns lighted. The trick worked. The attack was launched; the Turks were defeated. The besieged town was saved.

And John Smith was made captain of two hundred and fifty horsemen!

Captain John Smith! John whispered it to himself when no one could hear. To be a captain at twenty-one, to lead men into battle was more than he had dreamed possible.

He was in the midst of one of the bitterest wars ever fought. The Turks had invaded Europe. They had overrun much of Hungary and had taken its capital city, Buda. It was feared that they might conquer all of the Continent.

John Smith was sent with General Folta, his commander, to the east, into Transylvania. The country was overrun with armies of bandits. These men were under Turkish rule, but they fought only for themselves. They robbed the poor people of their food. They swooped down on villages and carried off women, crops, animals. They left a trail of hunger and misery wherever they went. To get rid of these lawless fighters was now John Smith's job.

But the bandits would not come out from their walled city and fight and Folta's men could not get into the city. Days passed. Folta set up camp on a plain and began to throw up piles of earth for the cannon. The bandits shouted and mocked them from the walls. At last one of their captains sent a challenge. He would fight in single combat against any captain the Christians would choose. Lots were drawn among Folta's officers, and John Smith was chosen!

When all the arrangements had been made, the bandit chief rode out onto the plain. His body was covered with armor, with a pair of great wings made of silver and eagle feathers fixed to his shoulders. Before him marched a soldier bearing his lance. On each side of his horse marched other attendants. Then, from the other end of the field, came John Smith. The two fighters met and saluted each other in the middle of the field. Then they rode back and waited.

It was John's first attempt at single combat. Now his life might depend on the things he had read in books of knighthood or learned at Tattershall.

The trumpets sounded. John put the spurs to his horse and lowered his lance. At just the right moment he made his horse swerve. His lance passed through the bandit's helmet, and killed him. Following the custom of the time, John, the victorious captain, cut off the head of his challenger and presented it to his general.

A friend of the dead man now challenged Smith, and he, too, died the same way. In order to gain more time for Folta to set up the cannon, Smith sent another challenge into the town. This time, the contest was fought with pistols and battle-axes. As John aimed a blow, his ax glanced off the bandit's armor. The weapon fell from John's hand to the ground. At the same moment a stroke from the enemy stunned him.

He slumped forward and almost slid off the horse. A cry went up from the crowd. Dazed, John leaned to the other side to recover his balance. He drew his broadsword, rode after the bandit and ran him through the body.

Thanks to the delay provided by these single combats, the Christian army had been able to raise earthworks and place cannon on them. The city wall was stormed and the entire bandit army captured, killed or driven away.

In gratitude to young John Smith, Prince Sigismund gave him rich presents and, best of all, a coat of arms. Now the young tenant farmer from England was a gentleman indeed!

After defeating the bandits, Folta's army was itself defeated by a huge force of Tartars. Hordes of skilled riders swept across the battleground killing the wounded and taking weapons and clothing from the dead.

John Smith lay on the ground, too sorely wounded to move. The Tartars took his armor but decided to spare his life, knowing that he would bring a good price on the slave market.

Chained together with nineteen other captives, John was forced to march all the way to the Turkish capital of Istanbul. There he was sold to a young noblewoman who sent him as a gift to her brother across the Black Sea.

The brother was the ruler of a small section of the great Turkish empire. He had John stripped, his hair and beard shaved off, and an iron collar riveted around his neck. Then he put him to work with the rest of his slaves.

One day, while John was threshing grain, the master rode by. He fetched John a blow with his riding whip and shouted senseless abuse. John could stand it no more. Striking the man dead with his threshing bat, John took his fine clothes, jumped onto his horse, and galloped off into the desert.

He was a thousand miles away from the place where he had been captured. He could not speak the language of the people whose country he must pass through. If he was lucky enough to escape capture, he might die of hunger in the desert sands.

But luck was with him. Using the sun as his guide, he came at last to Russia. Here, his irons were struck off and he was supplied with food, money and clothes. Then he began the long journey to the West. In Hungary he found many friends who had thought him dead. He went on into Germany, France and Spain, still looking for a way to earn fame and fortune. Hearing that a soldier could find work to do along the Barbary coast in Africa, he set sail for the shores of Morocco.

Once ashore, John met an English sea captain who invited him out to his ship to have dinner. A storm came up, and the ship had to put out to sea to avoid being driven on the rocks. Like many a captain in those days, the sea captain was not above seizing a ship if it belonged to a country unfriendly to England. When the storm was over he caught up with a Spanish vessel and took it, along with the valuable cargo aboard. John Smith saw that this unexpected voyage was not going to be without danger and excitement.

They passed small vessels flying the Spanish

flag but did not challenge them. Then came two imposing ships which looked to be rich prizes. Too late, the Englishmen saw them to be Spanish men-of-war.

There was a fierce struggle. The English ship caught fire and twenty-seven seamen aboard were killed.

John had seen enough fighting for awhile. As soon as the battered ship limped to a safe harbor, he took passage on a merchant vessel for England.

The wide world the farmer's son had seen so long ago from the Willoughby church tower had provided adventure indeed. John had proved himself an able soldier and, more important, a man of courage and endurance. He had packed into a few short years enough experiences to last most men a lifetime. Would he ask for more?

America!

⏣ BACK HOME IN ENGLAND JOHN found little mention of the wars he had left behind in the East. Everyone was talking about America.

On the London docks, in the taverns, in the pit of the Globe Theatre where the plays of Christopher Marlowe and of William Shakespeare were the rage, the talk was all about the New World. In front of Saint Paul's Cathedral little else but the land across the Atlantic Ocean was spoken of.

Saint Paul's was the place where men went to swap news. The gossip in front of the cathedral took the place of a newspaper. Sailors who had just returned from long voyages loitered there, always sure of a crowd willing to listen to their tales of adventure. Men in search of work went there to look for employers. Lawyers met their clients and tailors went to study the latest fashions worn by young lords and dandies.

Captain John Smith, fresh from Turkey and Russia and Morocco, had plenty of adventures to recount that would have tickled the crowd. But for once he preferred to listen.

"All their dishes are pure gold?"

"Their streets are paved with it. The children play with lumps of gold instead of stones."

"Yes, and you could live there like a free man with no lawyers prying into your business. You could till your land without saying 'by your leave' to a lord."

John had had enough of the wars in Europe. God had saved his life, brought him through all kinds of dangers. Now he wanted to give his life to a cause that would be worth fighting for.

To establish in the new world an English colony, with land any farmer could own! There was a thing he had long ago dreamed of. Now he gave his whole heart to it. None of the heroes in those stories of knighthood, which John had loved so much, had attempted anything grander than that.

But how did you get to America?

John began asking questions. At last he heard rumors about a company of settlers being formed to sail to Virginia. The Merchant Adventurers were going to send out men to set up a colony.

First they would have to get permission of King James, the new ruler who had come to the throne. Then ships had to be chartered, colonists chosen. Edward Wingfield, one of the agents of the Virginia Company, was willing enough to enroll the young captain fresh from the wars; but he could not say when the expedition would be ready to set sail.

Months went by and nothing seemed to be happening. John was tired of waiting. He was young and full of energy. He wanted action. Besides, his purse was getting lighter all the time.

At last, one day in April, 1606, he met Wingfield in front of Saint Paul's Cathedral.

"Captain Smith, I have news for you," the gentleman said. "The King has granted us a royal charter. We'll sail as soon as we can get ships."

John's face lit up. "I'm at your service, sir," John said.

But it was eight months before the three ships were ready to sail, with Christopher Newport as captain. During the reign of Queen Elizabeth, Newport had made many voyages to American waters. As a privateer, he had captured or destroyed more than twenty Spanish ships carrying gold from America to Spain. It was no wonder, then, that he and the men with him, now starting out to America, expected to find gold there.

The colonists numbered more than a hundred men and boys. Among them were carpenters, bricklayers, a parson, a barber, a tailor, a cobbler, and twenty-nine gentlemen who had done no work in their lives and intended to continue to live in idleness on vast new lands in Virginia. There was not one among them who did not expect to be named on the governing council, though how many and which names had been chosen was a secret until the end of the voyage.

On the twentieth of December, Newport's flagship, the *Sarah Constant,* pulled up her anchor and with the red cross of England flying at her masthead, started down the River Thames. Behind her, like ducklings behind their mother, came the smaller *Goodspeed* and *Discovery*. The *Discovery* was a tiny thing of only twenty tons—a small ship for a voyage of three thousand miles.

John Smith stood at the rail of the *Sarah Constant*, with his feet wide apart, short but sturdy. He wore a beard, now, that came down to a point at his chin, and a handsome moustache. He had thrown his brocaded velvet cape back from his shoulders. One hand rested easily on the hilt of the sword which hung at his side. No one now would think it ridiculous, as Robert Bertie had, to call this man "Captain."

He watched London fade in the distance. Then he walked forward to the bow of the ship. The long waiting was over. He was riding toward adventure again!

But the ships had barely passed the river's mouth when they had to anchor to wait for a favorable wind. When a wind came, it blew the wrong way. The ships tossed and rolled. The men were damp and cold. The food was not too good, the water began to taste stale. For six weeks the ships were anchored within sight of England. Tempers grew short, quarrels broke out. There was talk of giving up the voyage.

Then suddenly the wind shifted. "Fair weather!" called the captain. "Man the yards. Out with all your sails!"

The great squares of canvas filled with wind. The water hissed along the sides. The wake spread out behind. The long voyage had begun.

John Smith saw little of the great ocean he had longed to cross. The voyage had barely got under way when a quarrel broke out between himself and Edward Wingfield.

Wingfield could never forget that he had been born a gentleman while John Smith for all his bold airs was nothing but the son of a tenant farmer. He could not abide the young man who thought himself as good as anyone else.

And John's temper was as quick as his courage. Was he not an experienced traveler? Hadn't he proved himself in single combat with the fiery Turks? Perhaps he spoke more bluntly than he should. In any case he soon found himself under arrest for mutiny, held prisoner deep in the hold of the vessel.

After three months the fleet reached the

West Indies. Men in canoes came gliding out from shore to offer pineapples, potatoes and other fresh food. For three weeks the ships sailed among the beautiful islands. Sailors and colonists alike went ashore in search of fresh food—birds, turtle, fish, eggs.

But John Smith, all this time, did not see daylight.

The ships headed north for Chesapeake Bay and Captain Newport was busy with his maps and charts. "We should see land tomorrow," he said after a week's sail from the West Indies.

They sailed three days, and still no sight of land. Newport said little, but he looked worried.

Captain Ratcliffe of the *Discovery* came aboard the flagship. "We're lost," he said, and he demanded that they sail back for England before they starved in mid-ocean.

At five o'clock that afternoon a storm struck the ships. They could do nothing but furl all their sails and try to ride it out. All through the night the wind howled and the little ships tossed and rolled. Four days later, when they had given up all hope, a sailor posted high in the rigging shouted, "Land ho!"

Suddenly, the decks were crowded with

men. They ran to the rails, shaded their eyes with their hands and stared across the water.

"There! There it is!" They shook hands, pounded each other on the back, talked with much excitement and little sense.

But John Smith had no share in the rejoicing. He was still in the brig charged with mutiny.

That evening all the men who could crowd onto the deck of the *Sarah Constant* gathered around Captain Newport. A sealed box was brought out which had been given him in London by the Virginia Company. In it were the names of the men who were to take charge of the colony once the ships reached America.

The box was broken open, the names read. There were only seven names on the list and one of these was John Smith. Wingfield held a whispered conversation with Captain Newport. John Smith's name was quietly ignored.

The next day, work began on a knocked-down boat, a shallop, which could be sailed or rowed up the rivers. On the last day of April the ships moved up to a place which the men named Point Comfort. Five Indians stood on the shore, watching.

"Man the shallop!" Captain Newport

shouted and had himself rowed to shore. When he stepped out on dry land and laid his hand on his heart in a gesture of peace the Indians dropped their bows. They motioned him and his party to come to their village.

At the settlement the Indians led the way to a lodge, brought mats and motioned the visitors to sit down. The brown-skinned men and women looked with grave wonder at the bright silks and velvets. The Englishmen looked with equal interest at the bird's legs, feathers or pieces of copper which adorned the Indians' headdress.

Baskets full of food were passed around, then a pipe of tobacco. Finally, the Indians jumped up and with a frightening howling and stamping began a dance.

For two weeks the English sailed the little shallop up and down the river, looking for a good place to establish a town. But John Smith, a prisoner aboard ship, had no part in all this.

Finally, on the thirteenth of May, 1607, the larger vessels came to anchor in the river the settlers called the James, after their king. Six of the seven members of the council were sworn in. They chose Wingfield as president.

But John Smith was still kept below, a prisoner.

The next day he was allowed to go ashore. Happy to be on land again, he joined in the work of cutting trees, pitching tents, planting a garden. The other members of the council did no work. They busied themselves with planning a fort.

A hundred Indian warriors visited the new settlement with their chief. One of the warriors stole a hatchet. An Englishman grabbed it back and struck the thief on the arm. A second Indian ran up with raised club. The English reached for their muskets. Only the Indian fear of English guns prevented a battle.

John Smith pressed his lips tight and shook his head. He knew the men should be drilled so that they could take care of themselves, but at the same time should avoid starting a fight. He knew the fort ought to have strong walls instead of the few boughs of trees thrown up in a half circle. But it was for the leaders to give orders—not for plain John Smith. He was still kept from his rightful place on the council.

A few days later he was surprised when Captain Newport invited him to go with twenty others to explore the river, in small boats. Wherever they stopped, the Indians were friendly. They brought out food and tobacco. They danced, and made long speeches which the English, of course, could not understand.

But when the explorers got back to Jamestown, they found that the place had been attacked. A young boy had been killed and a man was dying. Fourteen had been injured. Too late to save the lives of those who had been killed, the colonists had begun to build a strong wall of logs and to bring cannon from the ships.

At last Wingfield decided that John Smith should be given his rightful place in the council. His military skill was plainly needed to drill the men.

The members of the little colony were called together. Short and sturdy, his head high and his back stiff and straight, John Smith took the oath: "I shall faithfully and truly declare my mind and opinion according to my heart and conscience in all things treated of in the council."

The words of the oath were easy to say. But it was going to take a big man to live up to them.

A Girl Named Pocahontas

CAPTAIN NEWPORT'S ORDERS had been to stay two months in the country and to explore for gold and for rivers leading to the Pacific. Then he was to return to England, leaving the settlers to build a town.

Neither gold nor a waterway to the Pacific had been found; but already the food supply was dangerously low. On June twenty-second, Newport sailed for London, promising to come back in twenty weeks.

As the ships sailed down the river, John Smith turned to look at Jamestown. The three-sided fort was only half finished. But guns were mounted at each corner. A few rough buildings had been erected inside, but some of the men still had to sleep in tents. Others slung hammocks in the trees. John shook his head. It was not good enough.

He walked up to a group of gentlemen who were sitting idly on a log.

"Come—let's get to work on the wall," he said.

The men went on talking and laughing.

"Until this fort is finished, we could be wiped out by Indian attack," the little captain insisted.

Still the men paid no attention to him. John felt his anger rising. For weeks these men had idled and complained and wasted time. Yet their lives depended on finishing the fort. It was clear, now, that many of them had come to America only because they hoped to find easy riches or to escape trouble at home.

John grabbed the largest of the gentlemen and pulled him to his feet.

"It's high time you started to earn your food," he said. "I'm going to fight every man who refuses to work—with sword, pistols or my bare hands. Now march."

And John saw to it that the men kept at

work all day. No one was allowed to shirk.

The fort was almost finished when a dangerous fever attacked the camp. Soon everyone was sick. By September nearly half were dead. The others tried hard to finish the wall of logs. It was more important than ever now that the colony was so weak in numbers.

One morning, when John tried to get up, his head started spinning. For days he was too sick to move. In his fevered dreams he imagined that he saw Indians pouring through the gap in the log wall. He tried to get up to fight them, but was too weak to rise.

When at last he was well enough to get up, he found that there were only five men in the whole camp strong enough to handle a gun. Captain Gosnold, one of the council, was dead. Kendall, another member, refused to work with the other members and was dropped. Wingfield had turned out to be a poor president. Smith, Martin and Ratcliffe went to his tent and informed him he was no longer president or a member of the council.

"You have eased me of a great deal of care and trouble," he answered.

John Smith was now put in charge of all outdoor affairs. He found the tents rotten, the houses still unfinished. The food supply was so low that each man had only a dish full of boiled wheat and barley a day. The men were so weak from sickness and so full of despair that they would do nothing to help themselves.

John called together all who could get up from their beds. They were a gaunt, unshaven, sad-looking group.

"If we go on this way, we'll all soon be dead," he told them. "We came out here to plant a colony for England. It's been tried before. Sir Walter Raleigh tried it and failed. But the Spaniards have done it. So can we. Everything worth having is hard to get—remember that. Now—the first four men over there, go and cut us some tall grass for thatch. The next four, bind it into bunches. You men here, come with me. We'll cut enough trees to roof those houses before the day is out."

Before nightfall the men had done more work than in the week past. As they returned from their work that evening, they heard a honking in the sky.

"Wild geese!" John said. Tired as he was, he loaded his musket with small shot and crept down to the water's edge. When the birds flew down, he and a few other men shot enough for a feast. When they got home, they found that Indians had brought a gift of corn. The men who had ridiculed John Smith because he was small or because he worked so hard began to look at him with new respect.

When the food supply ran out again, John Smith took six or seven men in the shallop and went down the river to an Indian settlement to trade beads and knives and hatchets for corn. But the Indians wanted weapons. They knew how badly the English needed food. So they offered corn for a sword or a musket. John Smith was determined they should have no English arms.

The orders from London were to have no fights with the Indians. But the English had to have food to survive.

"We'll see whether they'll trade or not," John said. "Run the boat ashore." As the boat pulled in to shore, John fired his musket into the air. At the sound the Indians fled into the woods. John and his men walked

into their village where corn lay in heaps.
The men put down their muskets and started
to gather the corn in their arms.

"Not yet," John said. "They'll attack us
soon. When that's over, we'll see if they'll
trade. But we'll not steal their corn."

In a few minutes sixty or seventy Indian
warriors came out of the woods. Their
bodies were painted black or red or white.
Some had all three colors. The stripes on
their faces gave them a terrifying appearance.
The noise they made was terrifying, too. One
of them carried a kind of doll, an image
made of animal skins and hung with chains.
The rest had clubs or bows and arrows.

John and his men fired their muskets. The
Indians turned and ran back into the woods,
leaving their image behind. John picked it
up and waited.

Soon a lone Indian stepped out of the
woods, unarmed. He walked toward the
river. John strode forward to meet him,
holding out some beads in his hand. By
signs he let the Indian know that he wanted
only friendship and trade. Let them load his
boat with corn and he would give them back
their image, he said. He would give them

beads and copper and hatchets besides. Somehow, though he knew no word of their language, he made himself understood.

In a few minutes a whole line of Indians came marching down to the boat. They brought corn and bread made of corn. They brought venison and wild turkeys. When they had loaded the boat, they stepped back onto the shore. Captain Smith passed over their precious image and the promised gifts. As the Englishmen took up their oars they could hear the Indians singing and dancing on the shore.

For a while the men at Jamestown had enough to eat. But John knew that a long winter lay ahead of them. So he made several trips up and down the river to get more corn. Everywhere he went, he heard about the great chief, Powhatan, who was king over all the tribes. If the English could make friends with Powhatan, John thought, there would be no problem about getting food.

In November he set out again, taking eight men with them. He sailed up the Chickahominy River until the shallop could go no farther, then persuaded two Indians with a canoe to take him and a couple of his men still farther.

"Don't leave the boat while I'm away," he cautioned those who remained behind.

The canoe glided twelve miles up the narrowing stream. Boughs and trunks of trees had fallen close to the water. The travelers had to duck under them as the canoe pushed forward.

The river ended in a marsh. The men were hungry now. John set the two Englishmen and one of the Indians to boiling corn, while he and the other Indian hunted birds. He had been gone only a short while when shouts echoed through the forest. Quickly he bound the Indian's arm to his own wrist. If there had been treachery, he did not intend to let the man get away.

A moment later an arrow struck him in the leg. He turned in time to see two painted warriors drawing their bows. When he fired, they fled. But before he could load his pistol, four more Indians had appeared.

Holding his hostage in front of him, John kept loading and firing his pistol. He was able to keep the attackers at a distance. Their arrows stuck in his clothes but did him no harm. But at last two hundred braves formed a circle around him. They lay close to the ground with bows drawn.

They called on Captain Smith to give up his arms. They made it clear that all his party, both in the boat and the canoe, had been killed.

Could he hold them off while he worked his way back to the canoe?

He stepped back, lost his footing in the swampy ground, and fell into the mud. Now there was nothing he could do but throw his pistol aside and hope for the best. When he climbed out of the cold, half-frozen mud, the Indians gathered around him.

Boldly he asked for their captain. A tall, befeathered warrior stepped forward. He was Opechankanough, brother of Powhatan.

To gain time, John Smith took out a compass, and presented it to Opechankanough. The Indians were fascinated by the motion of the needle. Even more, they were fascinated by the fact that they could see it but not touch it. This was their first experience with glass.

Finally the warriors grew tired of this new toy. They tied John to a tree, gathered around him in a circle, and prepared to shoot him full of arrows. But the chief held the compass up and spoke sternly. The braves put down their bows, untied their prisoner, and led him to a village of thirty or forty houses.

Men, women and children came running to see the captive and formed a ring around him. The warriors began a dance, yelling war cries as they moved around their prisoner. Then they led him into a long house where they offered him enough corn bread and venison for twenty men.

After a few days John had learned to understand a little of the Indian's language and to speak a few words. The warriors told him, with a flourish of their hatchets, that they were going to attack Jamestown. They offered to make him a brave and give him land and an Indian wife if he could help.

"The cannon will kill you all," John answered. "And then my friends will destroy your village."

He offered to write a letter to Jamestown to say that he was safe. This, he said, would keep the English from attacking with their guns. In the letter he also asked for several things he needed. The Indians who carried the letter were amazed when everything happened just as he had promised, and the articles he had sent for were given them. There was magic in the "speaking paper"! Their captive was plainly an important chief.

Now Smith was taken on a tour up and down all the rivers. Every Indian village wanted to have a look at the great white chief. But still he had not seen Powhatan.

A new year had begun before he was finally led to Weromocomoco, Powhatan's village. There he was taken into a long house made of poles and bark. Rows of men and women lined the building.

At one end a fire was blazing; nearby, on a platform, sat a handsome-looking man with gray hair and a hard-muscled body. A great robe of raccoon skins fell from his shoulders and spread out around him. At last John was in the presence of the great chief, Powhatan.

As he entered, all the people gave a great shout. John Smith stood in their midst, not knowing whether they planned to receive him as a guest or kill him.

* * *

The long house seemed to be bursting with people. The firelight shone on the red paint which covered the faces and shoulders of the warriors. John Smith marched to the front of the house where the fire burned. He kept his head up and his shoulders square, and looked boldly across the fire to where Powhatan sat. Then he bowed and spoke a few words in the Indian tongue.

"Why have you come to our country?" Powhatan asked him.

"Our ship was leaky, so we had to come ashore," said John Smith.

This explanation seemed to satisfy. Food was brought out and everyone ate as much as he could. Then the lesser chiefs gathered around Powhatan. It seemed as if their talk went on for hours and John could not make out what was being said. At last two great stones were brought in and placed in front of Powhatan. Strong hands seized John Smith and forced his head down against the stones. Others stood over him with clubs, waiting the signal to strike.

But the blows did not come. John heard a girl's voice and a gruff answer from Powhatan. Then he felt young arms about his neck. The men with clubs fell back. He looked up. A girl of thirteen was looking gravely at him with dark, wondering eyes.

"Thank you," he said in her own language. "I will never forget what I owe you."

A smile touched her face, the way sunlight strikes a forest floor when the boughs move.

"It is the wish of my daughter, Pocahontas, that you live," said Powhatan slowly. "She wishes you to make bells and beads and mirrors for her."

This was no time to explain that an Englishman did not make all his own things the way an Indian did. "She shall have bells and beads and mirrors," said John Smith. He spoke as calmly as if death had not been minutes away.

* * *

Two days later, Captain John was led to a long bark house in the woods and left there alone, sitting on a mat by the fire. The part of the house behind the fire was hidden by woven hangings of straw. Suddenly, from behind the curtain, a horrible noise was heard. Powhatan and all his braves rushed out, with blackened faces.

There was no Pocahontas to save John this time. He sat erect and looked straight ahead. When the blow fell, these barbarians would see that the English captain was not afraid.

The shouting stopped. "You are my son now," Powhatan said. "Your name is Nantaquod. I will give you land and you will give me, your father, a grindstone and two guns."

Then Powhatan sent John, through the crisp winter morning, to Jamestown. Twelve guides went along to bring back the presents for the chief.

The men at the fort welcomed Smith back with shouts and firm handshakes. They had missed his leadership. The ragged settlers looked warily at the Indian warriors but Captain Smith let the visitors into the fort and showed them a huge millstone and two heavy cannon.

"These are for Powhatan," he said grandly, knowing of course that they were too heavy for the Indians to move through the forests. "Here—let me show you how they work."

He loaded the cannon with stones and aimed into a tree from which great icicles were hanging. When icicles and boughs came tumbling down, the Indians ran away in fright.

Smith called them back. In place of the cannon which they could not carry, he gave them axes and beads and pieces of copper. Then he made a special package of beads and little bells, thread and scissors and mirrors.

"This is for Pocahontas," he said.

Exploring the New World

⊂Ε WHILE JOHN WAS AWAY, Captain Ratcliffe had named Gabriel Archer onto the council though he had no right to do this. Archer had studied law in London and had a reputation for being very shrewd in legal matters. Now he accused John of being to blame for the death of the men who had sailed upriver with him. He insisted on a trial and demanded that the little captain be hanged.

There is no telling how the matter would have turned out. But, at the moment that Archer was spouting his accusations in his best legal language, Captain Newport sailed into the bay from England. The trial was forgotten in the wild rejoicing of the twenty-eight survivors at the fort.

Now there was feasting on good English food, fresh news from home and men to take the places of those who had died. Captain Newport reported that another ship, the *Phoenix,* was also on its way with food and men. Altogether there would be a hundred and twenty new citizens for Jamestown. Among them was a new man for the council, named Matthew Scrivener.

However, the troubles of the colony were not over. A few days after Newport's arrival a man ran from his house, yelling "Fire! Fire!" In a moment the whole town was full of smoke. Flames leaped up from one roof of dry grass to another. Soon the roofs fell in and set everything else afire.

Men ran down to the river with buckets. But the fire was out of control. They could not even save their clothes. Mr. Hunt, the parson, lost his fine library. Within a few minutes Jamestown was a heap of ashes.

The newcomers were not hardened to living without shelter. Before new houses could be put up many grew sick and some died.

Pocahontas came often to visit John Smith, bringing gifts of food. When he saw the lovely Indian princess, Captain Newport wanted to meet her father, Powhatan. At last, in February, Captain John led Newport down the James River and into the broad waters of Chesapeake Bay. Then they sailed up the York River to Powhatan's town. To make sure that the way was safe, John took twenty men into town while Newport stayed aboard ship. Powhatan welcomed Smith in the long house and invited him to sit at his side.

John ordered presents brought for Powhatan—a suit of red cloth, a hat, and a greyhound.

"Where is your father?" Powhatan asked. "Is he not with you?" Smith had used the word "father" to describe Newport.

"He will come to you tomorrow," John answered in Powhatan's own tongue.

He and Powhatan began to bargain with each other. John wanted food and land. Powhatan said the English should lay aside their arms. John said only an enemy would ask this, but he did promise to help Powhatan defeat his enemies.

The bargaining was still going on next day,

when Newport with great ceremony came ashore. A man blowing a trumpet marched in front of him up to Powhatan's house.

For three or four days the Indians made a feast. There was dancing and trading. Newport gave Powhatan an English boy named Thomas Savage to live with him as a son. In return, Powhatan gave an Indian named Namontack to travel to England and back on Newport's next voyage.

But John Smith was worried at the way the trading was going. Newport's sailors traded too cheaply. This was going to make it difficult for Smith to get enough food for the colony.

Now Powhatan said shrewdly to Newport, "You and I are great chiefs. We must not trade for trifles. Lay down all the things you have to trade and I will give what I think they are worth."

John Smith had always refused to do this. He knew that the lives of his men depended upon keeping the price of his goods high. But Newport fell into the trap.

To set matters right, John Smith pulled a few beads out of his pocket.

"What are those?" Powhatan asked.

"These? Why, they're sky-colored beads.

Only the greatest of our chiefs wear them."

"I will give you a basket of corn for them."

Smith stuck them back in his pocket. "I'd rather keep them for myself," he said.

Of course, Powhatan felt that he had to have them. In the end, John got two or three hundred bushels of corn for a pound or two of glass beads.

After their return to Jamestown, Newport spent a month looking for gold. He never found any, but the seamen from his ship ate up a good deal of the food that should have been left for the colony. John was glad when, in April, Newport sailed for home, taking the troublemakers, Winfield and Archer, with him.

Ten days later, the *Phoenix* arrived from England, bringing a good supply of food and tools and several colonists from Holland who were skilled at building. When the *Phoenix* set out on its return voyage a month later, Martin was aboard. Only Smith, Scrivener, and Ratcliffe were on the council now.

Ratcliffe had wounded his hand and was not much use. Scrivener was a newcomer. Most of the work of leadership fell to John Smith. He saw to it that the burned fort was rebuilt. A new church was put up, a new roof on the storehouse.

John Smith was here, there and everywhere. He saw to it that the work parties had the tools and materials they needed, that fields were cleared and planted. He kept track of the food supplies. When Indians came to the fort to trade, he bargained with them. After all its troubles, Jamestown began to enjoy good times.

One day, a party of Indians walked into the fort, picked up some tools and started to walk off with them. The English had already lost many tools. When John tried to stop these men, they began to fight.

"Shut the gates!" John shouted. He drew his sword to defend himself and drove the Indians to a corner of the wall.

The rest of the Indian party outside the gates now began to yell and threaten. John mounted the wall and shouted down at them, "When you bring back the things you have stolen, your friends will be set free."

The warriors loitered uncertainly outside the fort until nightfall. Then they disappeared.

The next day Pocahontas came to the gate and was quickly let in. John Smith's eyes lighted up at the sight of her slim, graceful figure and her dark eyes. "Welcome, child," he said. "What brings you here?"

"My father wants his men back."

"And he has sent you for them?"

"He has."

"There is nothing you can ask of me that I can refuse," said John in a voice far gentler than the one he used with his men. "Can you bring back the tools and weapons they have taken?"

"I will try."

"Then the prisoners we hold are yours. And so are these if you like them." He drew some metal bracelets from his pocket and slipped them on her wrist. He watched the dark light glow in her eyes, and he looked at the soft curve of her chin as she looked down, admiring the gift. He stroked her black, straight hair with a friendly hand. The life of soldiering had not left much chance for tenderness. He had lost touch with his family. Pocahontas was all he had that was warm and tender in his life, and he loved her as if she had been a little sister.

"Go then, child," he said. "Tell Powhatan that we send the men back because you ask it."

The smile like forest sunlight crossed her face. John stood and watched her as she slipped out the gate.

*   *   *

John Smith stood at the bow of the barge, an open sailing boat, and watched the white eastern shoreline of Chesapeake Bay grow closer. Often he looked at the compass in his hand. Sometimes he added lines to the map he had fixed to a board. The map showed all the rivers, all the Indian towns in the Chesapeake Bay area. That is, it showed all he had visited. To complete the map, he was sailing all the way up into the bay.

This was the work he loved. To go where no European had gone before, to sail up new rivers—this was living. Every turn of a river opened up a new scene. Every Indian village brought a new danger. What a big country it was! And how empty! John thought of the English towns that could be built here. Such a country as this could support thousands, maybe millions of people. His little dream of winning a piece of land for himself had grown into a great vision.

"And I'm going to bring them here," he told himself. That would be his life work— to bring England to America, to make towns rise up in the wilderness, to make the wilderness safe and rich and happy.

For two weeks he explored river after river, filling in his map. At the mouth of the Rappahannock River there were so many fish that John began to spear them with his sword. Soon he had enough to feed all his men for a whole day.

The last fish he caught was a stingray. As he lifted it off his sword, the long, tailed sting drove deep into his wrist. Soon his hand was swollen, then his arm and shoulder. The pain stabbed like a knife wound. John was sure he had not long to live. His eyes, pinched with pain, rested on a peaceful-looking island.

"Bury me yonder on the island," he said. "Anas Todkill, you will be in charge. You'd best go back to Jamestown."

But one of the men in the party was skilled in medicine. He opened the wound and treated it with a precious oil. Soon the pain grew less. By supper time John was able to eat some of the fish he had caught.

Sailing back to Jamestown, he spent three days there. Then he headed up into the bay again. This time he mapped some of the streams he had not explored before. By the time he reached the top of the bay, most of his men had taken sick. Captain John himself was at the tiller when he saw eight Indian canoes ahead of him. They were filled with painted warriors who seemed to be looking for a fight.

He glanced at his men. Half of them were too weak to raise their heads.

"Those of you who can move—get to the sides," he said. "Take an extra hat and extra musket with you. If we look ready to fight, it may be we won't have to."

The Indians stared at the big boat with its high sides. They saw a whole row of hats and muskets. John stood high in the stern, the rudder between his legs, his musket ready. He was an easy target. But his trick fooled the Indians. They glided quietly by.

*   *   *

Now the boat sailed on up the bay and up the Susquehanna River as far as it could go. Still John was not satisfied. He had heard about the Susquehanna tribe of Indians and he wanted to meet them. He sent an Indian guide up the river to invite the leaders of the tribe to visit him.

After three or four days, sixty Susquehanna braves came gliding down the river in their canoes. They were big men—to John they

seemed as big as giants. They brought presents of venison, baskets, bows and arrows, and tobacco pipes three feet long. In return, John Smith gave them beads and copper and pocket knives.

The big men watched while the English had their daily prayer and Bible reading. Then they raised their hands to the sun and began to chant prayers of their own. Next they put their hands on the captain and bowed to him. They put a huge bearskin robe on him and a heavy necklace of white beads around his neck.

The voyage continued. John Smith was doing more than make a map. He had never given up the hope of finding a river which would lead to the Pacific Ocean. No one knew how big America was, and the English hoped to find a short passage to China and India. If they could find it, they, instead of the Spanish and Portuguese, would control the rich trade with the Orient.

John Smith was also looking for something which could be shipped back to England. The Merchant Adventurers who had put up the money to settle Virginia were getting impatient. The Spaniards had found gold in America. Why couldn't the English?

Or if not gold, then something else of value. Perhaps furs, or glass or tar or some of the other things England had to buy from other countries.

Virginia did have something which would bring gold to England. But it was years before anyone realized that Virginia's gold was only a weed—the golden leaf the Indians smoked in their pipes.

Can Jamestown Survive?

◖ JOHN SMITH RETURNED TO Jamestown from his long voyage on the seventh of September. Three days later he was elected president of the council. This recognition of his leadership by Scrivener and Ratcliffe gave him the power to carry out some of the things that needed to be done.

The first thing he did was to make Jamestown bigger. He added two sides to the fort and built better houses. He divided the men into companies and had a guard on duty at all times. Every Saturday he held a drill.

The Indians in the neighborhood never tired of watching the military drill.

"Rest your musket!" Captain John would call. The men would fix their guns on a metal rest.

"Draw out your match!" The clumsy, smoking fuse was made ready.

"Try your match! . . . Guard your pan! . . . Present! . . . Give fire!"

When the musket balls hit the target set up on a tree, the little captain knew the Indians would understand the power of a gun.

In October, Captain Newport sailed in from England bringing more men and Jamestown's first women, the wife of Thomas Forrest and her maid, Anne Burrowes. He also brought a crown and robe for Powhatan, gifts from King James. He had orders to crown Powhatan in feudal fashion and give him presents from England's king.

"We have no time for such nonsense," Smith objected. "If we're not to starve this winter, we must trade up and down the rivers for corn now that the Indian crops are in."

"I must obey my orders," said Newport. "I shall need a hundred and twenty men when I visit Powhatan."

"We can't spare them. I'll go overland

myself with four men and try to bring the chief back here to get his crown."

But when John Smith reached Powhatan's village of Weromocomoco, Powhatan was on a visit thirty miles away. Pocahontas came running to meet her captain. She took him by the hand and led him to an open field. A troop of girls came at her call. They spread a mat for John to sit upon, and made a fire for him and his men.

"Wait here for us," said Pocahontas. Then she and all her companions slipped away among the trees.

Suddenly a frightful shrieking burst out. The men jumped up and grabbed their muskets or put their hands on their swords. But Pocahontas came running out of the woods again.

"There's nothing to be afraid of," she said. "No harm will come to you. You may kill me if any harm comes to you or your men."

Men, women and children came and sat by the captain as Pocahontas disappeared again into the woods. Soon the troop of thirty girls rushed out of the forest. Their bodies were painted in bright colors and strange patterns. Their leader wore a pair of buck's horns on her head. A skirt of otter's skin was wrapped about her waist and she held a bow and arrow in her hand. Was it Pocahontas? John Smith could hardly be sure.

With shouts and cries, they formed a ring around the fire, singing and dancing, jumping up and down and making strange noises. Then they led John and his men to the village, gave them a feast and a place to spend the night.

Powhatan returned the next day but he refused to go to Jamestown.

So John had to go back alone. He persuaded Newport that fifty soldiers would be enough to accompany them for the ceremony of crowning the Indian chief.

They dressed Powhatan in fine clothes, and put a scarlet cloak around his shoulders. They gave him the king's presents—a handsome bed, a metal basin and pitcher. Then they tried to get the chief to kneel so that he could be crowned in the manner of European kings.

But Powhatan refused to kneel. At last they got him to stoop a little by leaning hard on his shoulders. At the moment of crowning a signal was given to the soldiers in the boats. A volley of shots cracked and echoed. Powhatan jumped as if he had been hit.

John Smith explained that the shots were fired in his honor and nobody would be hurt. Captain Newport had carried out his orders, but John Smith regretted the wasted time.

When they returned to Jamestown, John took thirty men down the river to fell trees and make clapboard to send back to England. The men worked so hard that blisters rose on their hands. When the blisters hurt, they cursed.

"There'll be a can of water poured down a man's sleeve every time he uses such words," said John Smith. The cursing soon stopped.

When Newport sailed for England, he carried a cargo of clapboards and some samples of hemp for rope and herbs for medicine. He also took Ratcliffe, who had become unpopular. With another long winter ahead, the members of the little colony depended more than ever on Captain John Smith to keep them alive.

* * *

In spite of all his efforts to keep peace with the neighboring Indian tribes, Smith often ran into trouble.

By the end of 1608 Jamestown was short of food again. Just as John was wondering what to do next, a message came from Powhatan.

"Send me men to build me a house after the English style," he said. "If you will do this, and if you will give me a grindstone, fifty swords, some muskets, a cock and hen and some beads, I will load your ship with corn."

Captain John sent four Dutch workmen and ten Englishmen by land to Powhatan. Then he set out himself with forty-six men in the shallop and two barges. He would never give arms to Powhatan. He would have his workmen build a house for the chief. Then he would make the best bargain he could for food.

The first night out, he stopped with a friendly chief who warned him:

"Captain Smith, you will find that Powhatan will be kind to you. But do not trust him, and never let him get his hands on your weapons, for he has sent for you only to cut your throats."

The captain thanked his friend and left with him one of the English boys who had come over with the first ships. He wanted Sam Collier to learn the language.

The boats moved down the river and came

out into Chesapeake Bay. Gusts of wind began to blow in from the ocean. Ice-cold rain sprayed the chilled men. Then came a storm of snow, so thick that they could not see.

"We'll head for the Indian village at Kecoughtan," John shouted. The boats groped their way through the storm. At last they found the village. Half frozen, the men crowded into the warm, smoky huts.

"Welcome, welcome," said their Indian friends. Out came baskets and platters made of bark or wood. They were loaded with oysters, fish, venison, turkeys and bread made of corn. Sitting around the cheerful fire, John and his men had a feast while the wind howled outside. They stayed there a week while the storm raged. All that time they were kindly treated and well fed.

Now they started up the York River toward Powhatan's village. There were no settlements along the York where they could find friendly shelter. When night came, they had to tie their boats to trees. Then they went ashore and made huge fires. They slept around the fires on the cold ground.

At last, on the twelfth of January, 1609, they reached the town of Weromocomoco. But the river was frozen nearly half a mile out from shore. Captain John grabbed an oar and strode to the bow of the boat. He whacked and jabbed at the ice until it broke.

"Push her at the stern with your oars!" he shouted. Some of the men thrust their oars into the shallow water. Slowly the boat moved forward. But soon it stuck again. The ice piled up on both sides. The barge stuck fast.

A bitter wind blew across the river. The men shivered and beat their arms with their hands.

"Let us not lie here and freeze to death," said Captain John. "Over the side with you, and we'll walk ashore across the ice."

The ice broke under the weight of the men. They sank up to their waists in icy water. Thick, cold mud sucked at their shoes. Their breath came in gasps. But John Smith urged them on. Holding their muskets and powder horns over their heads, they plodded toward shore.

Powhatan welcomed them with a feast. But it was hardly finished when he began asking Captain John how soon he would return to Jamestown.

"You sent me a message to come to you, and to send you men to build you a house," said the captain. "We came at your request."

"In my message I asked for weapons. We have no corn to trade with you," Powhatan replied, "except for swords. For forty swords I could find forty baskets of corn."

"We will give you copper for corn, but not swords," John told him. "To show you my love, I sent men to build you a house when I should have kept them at home to build our own. Yet now that I am here, you pretend you never sent for me. As for swords and guns, I told you long ago that I had none to spare. I have only enough to keep my colony from want. Yet I will never steal from you or wrong you unless you use me badly."

Powhatan listened gravely. "Many tell me that you have not come for trade, but to possess my country and kill my people. That is why they fear to bring you corn. Leave your weapons in your boat, and then we shall know that you mean us no harm. Then I will spare you corn from my store."

But Captain Smith would not give up his weapons. That night he and his men slept in Powhatan's houses. The next day the old chief began to talk again.

"I have seen the death of my people three

times," he said. "I know the difference between peace and war as well as any man. I am old, and soon I must die. I would like to be sure that you and my people are friends.

"What good will it do you to take from us by force, when we will gladly trade with you? If you kill us, who will provide you with food? And why do you fear us? Do you think I do not know that it is better to eat well and sleep quietly with my family, to have copper and hatchets from you as a friend rather than to fly into the woods and be so hunted by you that I can neither eat nor sleep? If you would only come to us without your weapons, we would gladly trade with you."

"If we had intended you any harm," the captain answered, "we could have done it long ago."

Still Powhatan pressed him to send his arms away. John was therefore all the more certain that Powhatan meant to attack him. He got some of the Indians to break the ice so that his boat could get in close to take on the corn. He also sent for more of his men to come ashore. When Powhatan learned this, he retired to the woods with all the women and children of the tribe. But soon a messenger came back with a chain made of mother-of-pearl.

"Powhatan fled because he fears your guns," said the messenger. "If you wish him to return, send them away."

But John was not fooled. He forced the Indians to carry corn aboard his boats. But before the boats could push off, the ebb tide left them stuck in the mud. There was nothing to do but spend another night in Powhatan's village.

Hunched over a fire to keep warm, John dozed off. He woke with a start when someone put a hand on his arm. It was Pocahontas. She had come alone through the dark woods.

She put a finger against John's mouth. "No one must know I am here," she whispered. "My father does not trust you. He plans to send you a great feast and then kill you. You must go away—now, at once."

John drew some trifles out of his pocket. She pushed them away. "No, no. If anyone saw them, they would know I came to warn you." There were tears on her cheeks. "Now go quickly."

John reached for her hand. But she shook her head and slipped out into the dark.

Soon eight or ten Indians came with platters of venison and other food. They begged the captain and his men to put their guns aside and eat. But first he had them taste the food to be sure it wasn't poisoned. Only then did he allow his hungry men to eat. And he kept his musket close by.

Soon messengers came from Powhatan to see what had happened. Then, more messengers came.

John Smith kept his men on guard all night until high water floated the boats. Then at dawn he sailed off with his load of corn. But the Dutch workers who had been sent to build Powhatan's house remained behind. They were sure the Jamestown settlers would either starve or be killed by Indians and felt safer with Powhatan.

As soon as Smith had gone, Powhatan returned to his village. The old chief hurriedly sent two of the Dutchmen overland to Jamestown. There, they pretended that Captain Smith had sent them to get more muskets and tools and ammunition. In this way Powhatan got for nothing what he had been unable to get from Smith by trading.

*   *   *

Meanwhile, John Smith had sailed on to the

village of Powhatan's brother, Opechankanough. This chief said he would send word to
all his people so that they might bring in what
they had to trade the following day.

When John marched up to the village with
fifteen of his men, Opechankanough made him
a long speech of welcome. But even while he
was speaking, one of the Englishmen who had
been left with the boats came and whispered
to the captain:

"There are seven hundred armed fighting
men in the woods and around the chief's
house."

"You're sure?"

"I saw them myself, Captain."

When the chief had finished his speech,
Captain John said, "Even while you have been
bidding us welcome, your men have surrounded the house. I see your plot to murder
me, but I do not fear it. Instead of making
our men fight, let the two of us fight each
other. That island in the river is a good
place. The man who wins shall be master
over all our men. If you win, you may take
all my copper and weapons. If I win, I take
your corn."

"No—no fight. We are friends," answered
Opechankanough hurriedly. "See, at the door

is a present my men have brought for you. Step outside and they will let you have it."

"Don't go," whispered the soldier. "There are at least a hundred men outside the door, and thirty lying under a great tree with their arrows ready to shoot."

John turned to his men. "If that is so, let us fight like men and not die like sheep," he said. "Lieutenant Percy and Master West, keep the braves in the house here from escaping. Master Powell and Master Behethland, guard the door. I'll take care of this treacherous chief."

Captain Smith grabbed Opechankanough by his long lock of hair. He pressed a pistol to his breast and led him outside the house. "Now," he said, "have your warriors lay down their weapons."

Seeing their chief in danger, the Indians threw down their bows and arrows.

Still holding the chief by the hair, John said, "I see the great desire you have to kill me. Yet, because you once saved my life when you caught me in the mud, I will be kind now. You promised to fill my ship with corn and so you must, or I will fill it with your dead bodies. But if you will trade with me as friends, all will be as before."

Now men, women and children came crowding in to trade with the captain. For three hours the trading went on, until he grew tired and went back into the house to sleep, leaving some of his men in charge. When the Indians saw him asleep, they sent a party of warriors to beat him to death with clubs. If John Smith were dead, they thought, they could easily kill the others.

If one Indian had crept up quietly, John Smith would have been a dead man. But the Indians were afraid of him. No one of them would go alone. The noise the crowd made woke him up. Still half asleep, he grabbed his sword and struggled to his feet. When the Indians saw the sword, they hesitated. John's shouts brought some of his own men. Together, they beat the Indians out of the house. To prevent any further trouble, they held the chief and some of his men.

Just as the trading ended, Richard Wyffin arrived from Jamestown with a message for Captain Smith. Scrivener had taken ten settlers with him on a voyage to the Isle of Hogs where the pigs were kept. The boat had been upset in a storm, and all aboard had drowned.

"Tell nobody," John warned the messenger.

He knew that this news might discourage his men at a moment when they needed all the courage they had. And he knew that if the Indians learned it, they might try again to wipe out his whole party. As soon as his boats were loaded, he returned to Jamestown, bringing enough food to last until the next harvest.

Enemies Within

☞ THE DEATH OF SCRIVENER HAD left John Smith as the only member of the council. He called all the men together.

"You see that power rests wholly in me," he told them. "So you must obey this for a law. Anyone who will not work shall not eat."

He divided the men into small work groups and sent them off to fell trees, build houses, or do whatever work was required. Each man worked six hours a day. The rest of the day was spent in games and entertainment.

John found that a Chickahominy Indian

had been held prisoner because a pistol had been stolen. His brother had been sent to bring the pistol back from the man who had stolen it.

John went to look at the man. He was in a prison without food or heat.

"Give him food, and some charcoal for a fire," John ordered.

About midnight the brother returned with the pistol. But when they went to set the other one free, they found that he had smothered himself with smoke and had then fallen unconscious into the fire where he had been badly burned.

"He is dead! He is dead!" cried the brother.

But John pulled the prisoner from the fire and felt his pulse. "Will you promise to steal no more if I bring this man to life?" he asked.

The brother promised for all his tribe.

"Bring the chest of medicines," John ordered.

He gave the unconscious man strong medicines and dressed his wounds. In a little while the Indian's pulse grew stronger. He stirred and sat up. In the morning, after a night's rest, he was well enough to travel. John gave both brothers a piece of copper and sent them on their way. The news soon spread throughout the country that Captain Smith could bring the dead to life. All those who had ever stolen anything from the English now came running to Jamestown with it. At last, it seemed, the little colony would have peace and plenty.

Now spring came on again, and the warm sun brought new energy to the winter-pinched men. Forty or fifty barrels of tar and potash were made to ship to England. A well was dug, twenty houses were built, nets were made for fishing, and more boards were sawed.

John's driving energy kept all the rest going. He built a blockhouse to guard the narrow neck of land by which everyone must enter Jamestown. He started a fort across the river on high ground.

Then came a horrible discovery. The corn which they had packed in barrels was rotting. Hundreds of rats were rapidly eating up the rest. Jamestown again faced starvation.

The work stopped on the fort across the river. The building of Jamestown stopped. John Smith called the settlers together. There were not quite two hundred of them now. Their clothes were ragged, stained and faded. Many looked thin and gaunt. John Smith stood in front of them. He waited until they grew quiet.

"Our food supply is running short again," he told them. "The Indians, themselves, have no more corn, and will have no more till the next harvest. Thirty or forty of us have until now found the food for all the rest. Now every man will have to work to get his own. I have never had more from the supply than any one of you. But from now on, every man will have to gather as much as I do. Those who refuse to work will be put out of the fort and left across the river.

"Some of you think I ought to give up the colony and take you all back to England. We'll never give it up as long as I'm president. If we leave, the Spanish will take Jamestown. I'd as soon give them London.

"Ensign Laxon, you will take sixty men down the river to live on oysters. Lieutenant Percy will take twenty men with him to Point Comfort to catch fish. Master West will take another twenty up the river to the Falls, to hunt. Those of us who stay here will take care of the garden and get what we can by hunting or fishing."

There was plenty of sturgeon in the river. When the Jamestown people got tired of eating sturgeon boiled or fried, they dried it and mixed it with herbs. They made bread from a root the Indians called "tuckahoe."

Then, every few days, Pocahontas would lead a party of Indians bringing squirrels and turkeys and deer. She led them always to John Smith's house. He had nothing left to give her that she did not already have. But she would point to his sword or his boots or his hat. Then he would tell her the English word for it. Soon she knew many English words, and learned to put them together.

"Good morning, Captain Smith," she would say. "I bring you some venison." Then she would look out of her dark eyes and smile her warm, shy smile. And John Smith would praise her and teach her new words. She learned quickly and did not forget what she learned.

And John Smith had a good time teaching her. All day long, men were bringing their troubles to him. But Pocahontas was like a fresh breeze from the forest. When he talked with her, he could forget the dangers and troubles of Jamestown.

*   *   *

On the tenth of July a ship sailed up the river. The men of Jamestown crowded to the shore as soon as the strange vessel appeared.

For months John Smith had feared that a Spanish man-of-war might come to wipe out the colony. Now he shouted commands.

"Gun crews to your stations! Lieutenants, parade your men with muskets!"

But while they rushed to obey, the ship ran up the English flag.

Captain Samuel Argall stepped ashore. He had letters for John Smith from the Virginia Company and he had complaints. Why had Smith not filled the ships that sailed for England with valuable things from the New World? Why had he got into fights with the Indians?

Captain Argall said that the Virginia Company had collected more money and would soon send a whole fleet of ships to Jamestown. There would be men with their families and supplies. The great Lord Delaware would soon come to America himself as governor of Virginia. To the ragged, homesick men at Jamestown it sounded too good to be true.

A month later, four vessels sailed up the James River from England. Nine ships had set out. Among those which failed to arrive was the *Sea Adventure*, which carried the new leaders the Virginia Company had sent out to govern the colony with new instructions.

There was general rejoicing in the settlement but John Smith realized that he was in a fix. Among the first voyagers to step ashore were Archer, Ratcliffe and Martin. John had quarreled with them all and they had used the months on shipboard to talk against the little captain. All the men who now came ashore were looking for trouble.

The Virginia Company had appointed new governors, had sent new orders. The newly appointed leaders were not here. They were on the missing ship, but the late arrivals would not accept John's leadership. In September, his year as president of the colony would end. Yet there was no one in Jamestown who could legally take his place.

As the day came near, John named Captain Martin, the least hostile of the three, to the presidency. After trying the job for three hours, Martin handed it back!

Jamestown was too crowded, so John decided to send Martin with a company of men down the river to settle on land bought from the Nansemond Indians. He chose Francis

West, the brother of Lord Delaware, to lead a hundred and twenty men many miles up the river to build a new camp.

After a week or two John went to see how West was faring. He found the men without a leader and in miserable condition. West had quietly returned to Jamestown where he could be more comfortable!

The men he had left behind were camped on low ground where it would be easy for a flood to wipe them out. John Smith went to the Indians nearby and bought a piece of high ground with the fort and log houses the Indians had lived in. He named the place "Nonesuch" and moved the settlers to this healthier spot.

Part of the bargain he had made with the Indians was that the English would help them against their enemies. Instead of this, West's men stole corn from the Indians and robbed their gardens. The Indians complained to Captain Smith. "These men do us more harm than our enemies," they told him.

But the new settlers would not listen to Captain Smith. So he left them to look out for themselves and started home for Jamestown.

He had not been gone from the place an

hour before some of them, who had gone into the woods, were surprised and killed.

Now the remainder of West's men were willing to listen to Captain John. He sent most of them back to Nonesuch after making peace with the Indians. But he ordered six or seven troublemakers into his shallop. At Jamestown, he felt, he could keep them under control.

As the boat floated down the James River, John stretched out in the bottom to catch a few hours of badly needed sleep. As always, his pistol and his bag of gunpowder were close beside him.

Suddenly, a roar woke him up. He felt a terrible pain in his leg. Someone, perhaps a careless smoker, had touched off his gunpowder.

John's clothes were afire. To put out the fire he jumped into the river, but his leg had been badly burned. The wound made him helpless and he nearly drowned before his men could get him into the boat again.

They were a hundred miles from Jamestown. There was no medicine aboard, no way to treat the gaping wound, no way to give John Smith any relief from the terrible pain.

When Archer and Ratcliffe saw him return

so badly wounded, they made up their minds to take over the government from him. By now John Smith was too weak and miserable to fight back. Against all these learned and wealthy men, he could not help reminding himself that he was only the son of a tenant farmer. He felt that he had done the best that any man could have done to hold Jamestown together. Yet these men called him a blustering upstart.

Perhaps if he could get back to England, his wound could be treated. One of the ships was about to set sail for the return voyage. He went aboard.

But the ship was held for three weeks while Archer drew up complaints against Smith to send back to the Virginia Company. All this while, John lay helpless in his hammock.

At last, the vessel dropped down into the broad, sparkling waters of Chesapeake Bay and out into the Atlantic. John Smith crawled on deck and looked back at the wide waters, the low green shores, the beaches of gleaming yellow-white sand, at the land he had grown to love. He knew the rivers, the forests, the Indian villages. He hated to leave it all. He hated to admit defeat. He wished he might have seen Pocahontas once more.

Somehow, he promised himself, he would come back to America.

*   *   *

After John Smith left Jamestown, disaster struck it. Ratcliffe and many others were killed by the Indians. Archer died. West deserted the colony and sailed away.

All the hogs and chickens which had been raised under John Smith's orders were eaten up. Swords and guns were traded to the Indians for food and still the colony starved. Some men went and lived as slaves to the Indians in order to have food. Others tried to keep alive on roots and acorns.

The population of Jamestown when Smith was sent away had risen to the number of five hundred. In the next months it dropped down to sixty hungry, miserable creatures.

In May, 1610, the leaders who had set sail in the *Sea Adventure* appeared in Chesapeake Bay. They had been shipwrecked off the Bermuda Islands, and had had to build a ship before they could get to Virginia. A few days after their arrival, they decided that they could not hold Jamestown. On June 7 they all went aboard the ship to sail for England.

But before they reached the mouth of the river a boat met them. Lord Delaware was on his way with a fleet of three ships! The colony was saved after all. But the man to whom the colony owed its survival was three thousand miles away in London.

The fighter, the adventurer, was huddled over a desk day after day. John Smith had found a new weapon to fight with. He was defending Virginia not with a sword but with a stiff quill pen!

A New Weapon to Fight With

⏏ WHEN THE SEA VOYAGE WAS OVER
John Smith had limped up the London street
from the dock. His leg ached. His clothes
were ragged. But he was alive and he was
home on English soil.

"Hot peas! Hot peas!" called one of the
street peddlers.

"Hot fine oatcake!" called another.

The smell of fresh hot food was a treat to a
man who had eaten little but ship's food for
many months. That food was to be had for
the buying seemed a miracle after the years
of struggle to keep a colony from starving.

The solid buildings, the great span of London Bridge, the huge Tower rising stone on stone were a great marvel to a man who had struggled to build a hut of sticks and mud in the Virginia wilderness.

And the sounds of the city—the street cries —the bells—the thump of horses' hooves on cobblestones, the creak of wagon wheels were almost deafening to John's ears tuned for three years to rustling leaves and bird song.

The first thing John Smith did was to go into a tavern and get a good meal. Then he went to a shop where a twisted, bloody rag showed that he would find a barber. He had his hair washed and cut, and his beard trimmed.

Then he went to get himself a new suit of clothes. He looked in the tailor's mirror and scarcely knew himself. His full beard and moustache gave him a rather fierce look. His face was lined, his eyes sunken. But the new fashioned tight jacket with puffed sleeves and big starched collar fitted well enough for such a quick job.

With his broad-brimmed hat and a rapier by his side he looked well enough to confront the members of the Virginia Company to answer the charges against him. It was true

they had met with many disappointments and
their ships had brought home no profits. But
he himself had suffered wounds, sickness and
misery, all without one penny in pay or a
word of thanks.

He went his way with new energy, in a
hurry to visit the Virginia Company and give
them his side of the story of Jamestown.

The Company held its meeting in the home
of Sir Thomas Smith, the most powerful
merchant in England. John Smith tried to
explain to the comfortable gentlemen that
Virginia was different from Spanish America.

"You'll find no gold there," he told them.
"You can buy your tar and other ship's
supplies much cheaper in Sweden, or your
glass in Venice."

"Then what *can* we get out of Virginia?"
they asked him.

"A place for Englishmen to live! It's fine
fertile soil there, with great flowing rivers to
carry men and trading goods up and down
into the country. Towns and cities as big as
any in England will grow there. And England may become rich trading with them.
But there will be no quick profits."

The men who had put their money into
the Virginia Company wanted to get it back.

John did not make himself popular by telling them the truth.

The story went around London that Virginia was good for nothing. This made the captain mad, because he had seen Virginia and he loved it. The story also went around that John Smith had made a mess of things there. This made him madder. He had given three years and often risked his life to get a part of America for England. He could not bear to see it go for nothing. But what could he do, to stop all these rumors?

He could write a book. He called it *A Map of Virginia* because it had a fine map in it which he had drawn himself. He told about the rivers and animals and the things that grew there. He told about the Indians and their customs. And when he gave an example of their language, the sentence he wrote had this message:

"Bid Pocahontas bring two little baskets, and I will give her white beads to make a chain."

He had not forgotten the girl who had saved his life.

When the manuscript was finished, John set out to get it printed. London was full of printing presses. There was William Welby's shop at the Sign of the Swan in Saint Paul's churchyard. Saint Paul's churchyard was full of bookstalls with apprentices standing in the doorways calling: "What lack ye, gentlemen? See, a new book come forth. Buy a new book!"

But the printers in Saint Paul's would print nothing that was not entered for publication at Stationers' Hall. And members of the Stationers had shares in the Virginia Company. John Smith's honest picture of life in Virginia might keep people from buying tickets to the great lottery the Virginia Company was conducting. So the printers in Saint Paul's churchyard hesitated and John Smith took his *Map of Virginia* up to Oxford to be printed and stayed to watch the pages come off the tall hand press.

The book was in three parts. First came the map, beautifully drawn with every small stream and sunny island marked. Then there was a description of the country and its inhabitants.

"The mildness of the air, the fertility of the soil, and the situation of the rivers," he wrote, "are so propitious to the nature and use of man as no place is more convenient for pleasure or profit."

Lastly, Smith had written the story of the settlement and the part he had played in it. He attacked people like Ratcliffe and Newport "who with their great words deluded the world with strange promises," and "devoured the fruits of other men's labors."

While he was writing his book, he heard that the treaties he had made with Powhatan and the other chiefs had been broken, that fighting had broken out where peace had reigned. He complained about these things and defended his own way of treating the Indians with firmness but with justice.

While he was waiting for his book to be printed, John Smith kept thinking about America. He was in love with it. He wanted to go back.

But how could he get there? He had no desire to go back to Jamestown, to take up old quarrels. Every returning ship brought news of fresh disasters, of stern laws, of the scramble for land to grow the highly praised tobacco crop in which Smith had small faith. He heard that, during an outbreak of fighting with the Indians, Pocahontas had been brought into Jamestown a prisoner. No— Smith did not want to go back to the settlement he had helped to found.

America was a big place, however. The English sea captains who had gone farther up the coast spoke well of it. He determined to explore the coasts to the north.

At last he got four London merchants to put up the money for a trading voyage. He chartered two ships and made long lists of supplies that would be needed. Then he went from one merchant to another to buy them.

He hurried down to the ships to see that the supplies were properly stowed. At last, toward the end of February in 1614, he went aboard. With him was an Indian named Squanto who had been brought to England by Captain George Weymouth nine years before. Squanto at last was going home.

Captain John climbed up onto the high quarterdeck at the ship's stern, and nodded to the ship's master.

"Make ready to sail!" called the master. "Hoist your sails half mast high."

The two small vessels moved down the Thames and out into the ocean. John Smith sniffed the clean sea air. He heard the hiss of water along the ship's sides and felt the deck rise and fall beneath his feet. He felt like shouting with joy. A new adventure lay ahead of him.

When he had dreamed of adventure as a boy, he had thought of knights on horseback. In Hungary, he had been a knight on horseback. Then he had dreamed of making important discoveries in America—discoveries that would bring him honor and fame. But the times were changing. Now, when a man went in search of adventure, he had to look for something practical like fish or furs.

The ships reached a rocky, deeply forested coast, and the hunt for whales was on.

"We saw many and spent much time in chasing them," John Smith wrote, "but could not kill any."

Europe ate more fish than could be caught on that side of the ocean. There would be a ready market for all they could bring home. The voyagers turned to fishing.

John Smith was no fisherman. While the sailors fished, he set out with eight men in a small boat to explore the coast of "Northern Virginia." This was the sort of thing he loved to do.

With a large piece of paper tacked to a board, he carefully drew the coast as they went along. He put in the rivers and hills and islands and he noted the good harbors. He went thirty miles up the Kennebec River, admiring the fine trees and sweet springs. But the place he fell in love with was a place that Squanto called Massachusetts.

"The paradise of all those parts," Smith called it. He liked the fine harbor, the islands with corn growing on them, the groves of fine trees.

After Squanto left them to rejoin his own tribe, they coasted along, trading with the Indians for furs, which sold at a good profit in England.

They got more than a thousand beaver skins and some martens and otter. But the season was getting late and many of the Indians to the east had already sold their furs to French traders. Smith's men did not get as many furs as they wanted and dropped down the coast in their small boat to see what else could be found.

Carefully, John Smith mapped the country, noting every little landmark. His mind leaped ahead of mere trade. Again he dreamed of founding a colony—a plantation in the New World for men who would "plant that ground he hath purchased by the hazard of his life."

The languages John Smith had learned in the Jamestown area were useless to him in these northern parts. The tribes with whom the men traded seemed friendly and peaceful but without being able to talk with them there was always a chance for misunderstanding.

Leaving the ships to their fishing, John rowed ashore with a few men to trade. Forty or fifty Indians gathered about him, as he spread out his beads and mirrors and knives for them to see. One of them picked up a knife and ran off with it. John Smith drew his sword and ran after him, but the Indian darted into the forest.

When John turned to go back, he saw that fighting had broken out on the shore.

He dashed down the hill. "Get back!" he shouted to the sailors. "Charge your muskets while I hold them off!" He dashed toward the Indians, waving his sword. They could easily have surrounded him and killed him with a stroke of a hatchet. But his attack was so strong and so unexpected that it drove them back. No one wanted to step into the path of that sharp sword.

When the men had their muskets ready, John Smith began to move backward. "Launch the boat!" he called.

A flight of arrows hissed through the air. He twisted and turned to avoid them. When he reached the rowboat, his men shot off a

volley from their muskets. John pushed the boat off and jumped in. Then he sat down and started to draw his map again as if nothing had happened. An hour later, the Indians paddled out in canoes, bringing gifts and offers of peace.

After rounding the tip of land that curved like a fish tail out from Massachusetts, John Smith headed back for his waiting ships. He found that fifty thousand pounds of codfish had been taken. When one of the ships was fully loaded with salt fish, fish oil and furs, John hoisted sail for England.

Still more fish were drying on shore. He ordered Thomas Hunt to stay with the second vessel until the cargo was ready, and then to sail for Spain to sell it there. After John Smith had sailed, Hunt lured twenty-four Indians aboard with promises of gifts. One of these was Squanto come to see his English friends. When the Indians were all below decks, Hunt ordered the hatches closed. Then he sailed off to Spain and sold them as slaves.

Meanwhile, John Smith was making a quick voyage to England. In August he sailed into Plymouth Harbor. He was excited about the part of America he had visited. He wanted to go back there to start a colony.

A Colony of His Own

IN PLYMOUTH THERE LIVED A man who shared John Smith's feeling about America. He was Sir Ferdinando Gorges, commander of the King's fort. Three Indians brought to England by Captain Weymouth had lived with him for almost ten years. Sir Ferdinando had taught them English and learned much about their country from them.

For hours he questioned John Smith about "North Virginia."

"You say it's a good country. How is it that no one has been able to plant a colony there?"

"They have tried to settle too far to the north. Our fishermen go out to the Grand Banks. There the fishing is far out from shore. But where I would settle, the fishing is close to shore. See here." Smith drew out his map and spread it on the table in front of him. Sir Ferdinando followed his finger.

"Here, in the Massachusetts country, is the place to settle. The cod come here early in the season. They can be brought back to England earlier and so fetch a high price. The fishing vessels can take colonists to the country. These men can dry and cure the fish on shore. In this way the fishing ships will not need to take double crews.

"The ships can go back well loaded with fish," he went on. "But the colonists will live in the new land in happiness. What pleasure can be more than in planting vines, fruits or herbs, in building homes, ships and other works, to have their own boats upon the sea? There every man may be master and owner of his own labor and land—in time each port in England can have its counterpart in New England."

Sir Ferdinando dropped his fist on the table. "Good!" he said. "For ten years I've been waiting for the right idea and the right man to settle northern Virginia. If you can get your own men, I will get you a ship."

John Smith hurried up to London. He went to see all the merchants he knew. From them he collected two hundred pounds. He looked all over London for brave men who would go with him to America. Day after day, he went to Saint Paul's Cathedral. He went to the Globe Theatre across the river. There, between the acts of a play by Shakespeare, he talked about America to anyone who would listen.

At last he got five men to go down to Plymouth with him. But when they reached Plymouth, they found no ship at all. Sir Ferdinando had tried hard to get the money to charter one. But the Plymouth merchants knew how much money had been lost by the settlement at Jamestown. They knew that no one had been able to make a success of starting a colony along the northern coast.

Finally, Sir Ferdinando went to see the dean of Exeter Cathedral, Matthew Sutcliffe. He was a member of the London Virginia Company, and had been interested in America from the beginning. He wanted to talk with Captain Smith.

So, together, Sir Ferdinando and Captain

John galloped by horseback over to Exeter. The dean asked a good many questions. He was a good judge of men.

John Smith talked about America. He showed his map, and pointed out the best harbors. He explained how he would build a strong town that could not be taken by Indians.

"I will support your voyage, Captain Smith," the wealthy churchman said.

*   *   *

Soon a ship of two hundred tons was ready to sail. A smaller one of fifty tons was also chartered. Beside the sailors and fishermen, sixteen men and two boys were to go as settlers. They would stay in America and build a colony.

The two ships picked up strong winds the minute they left the harbor. The waves grew higher and higher. Each time the ship's bow hit a wave, a mountain of water fell on the deck. John Smith clung to the rail, searching the horizon for the other vessel. The second ship was nowhere to be seen. It took all a man's strength to keep from being washed into the sea.

"Go into the cabin!" the master of the ship shouted at John Smith.

But John shook his head. "You've got too much sail on!" he called. "This wind will blow your masts away."

"If we furl our sails, she'll turn broadside to the waves and capsize."

The wind howled still louder. It sang and shrieked in the masts and rigging. Soaked from head to foot, John Smith began to work his way down the steps from the quarterdeck. He heard a sharp crack, like the sound of lightning hitting. The sound was quickly followed by two more. He looked up just in time to see the three masts with all their sails and rigging falling toward the deck.

"Look out!" he yelled. But no one could hear him. The great mass of wood and rope and canvas plunged down, just missing him.

The ship shuddered from the blow and leaned heavily to one side. Unless all that dead weight could be cut away, the ship would sink.

John crawled to the ship's cabin. A box of axes was there. It had come aboard at the last minute and had not yet been put in the hole. Captain John grabbed one and worked his way back to the deck. He held it up so the sailors could see it. Then he pointed to the cabin.

He had to hold onto the rail with one hand to keep from being washed off the slanting deck. With the other hand he worked the ax. Soon twelve axes were at work. They chopped through the hundreds of ropes. They chopped at the broken ends of the masts. But it was slow work. Every wave threatened to wash the workers overboard. If the masts came free at the wrong time, they would crush all those on deck, and sweep them into the sea.

When the last rope was cut, a great wave broke over the ship. It took masts and sails and all and carried them clear of the ship.

Now a sailor crawled out of a hatchway and came to the master. "She's leaking badly, sir," he said.

A pump was set up and the men took turns at it. When the wind died down, a small mast was lashed to the stump of the old one. Slowly the crippled ship worked its way back into Plymouth Harbor. The other ship had not been heard from.

Sir Ferdinando and the Dean of Exeter fitted out another vessel, but this time it was a much smaller one of sixty tons. Carrying the sixteen settlers and fourteen sailors, it sailed on the twenty-fourth of June.

They had sailed for a few days before a strong wind when they found that they were being followed.

"A pirate! A pirate!" shouted one of the sailors.

Chambers, the ship's master, crowded on all the sail he had. But the pirate ship came closer.

"Send us your dory. We're coming aboard you," the pirate captain called.

"Send your own boat if you want to come aboard," Chambers shouted.

"We've lost it."

Meanwhile, John Smith studied the pirate ship. Thirty-six guns it carried. He knew that it would be useless to put up a fight.

"What do you want of us?" he called.

"We'll tell you that after we see what you've got."

"We're heading for America to settle an English colony. I'll blow up the ship before I'll give up anything that would spoil our plan."

"All right. Send us your boat."

John Smith returned to his cabin. Soon there came a knock at the door, and in burst half a dozen of the pirates. They began pumping his hand.

"Don't you remember us, Captain Smith?" said one. "We were your men in Hungary. We'll sail to the Azores with you if you like —or to America."

John Smith was in a tight spot. He knew these were good men. They would be useful to him in America. He must not anger them or they might take the supplies he needed. Yet he could not spoil the reputation of his colony by doing business with pirates. He gave them some presents of food and a few other supplies they needed. Then he sent them back to their ship and they sailed away.

*   *   *

A day or two later the lookout called: "Two sail off the starboard bow!"

More pirates, this time flying the French flag.

"If they try to board us, we'll fight," said Smith.

"We were hired to fish, not to fight," said Chambers. "If we resist them, they'll toss us all into the sea."

"You'll defend this ship, or I'll split her open under your feet," said John Smith. "Man the guns."

After a few exchanges of cannon shot, the French ships sailed away. Still, there was no peace on the sea. Four more French men-of-war came up over the horizon. This time the odds seemed too great even for Captain Smith.

"Come aboard and show us your papers," the French captain called. "We are only after Spanish and pirate ships. If your papers are in order, we will not disturb you."

Nevertheless, after John Smith had gone aboard they held him.

For five or six days the five vessels traveled together. Meanwhile Captain John persuaded the French captain, Poyrune, to give him back his ship with all its supplies.

Many of the supplies had been taken onto the French ships. With a few men to help him, John Smith went back and forth collecting muskets and powder, bedding and ship's instruments. He was on one of the French ships when a sail was sighted. Off they went in chase of it.

The next morning Chambers drew alongside the French ship. He sailed so close that he split his sail on one of the yards.

"Captain Smith!" he called. "Come aboard or I'll leave you."

"Send the boat for me!"

"She's split," Chambers lied. "Come in their boat if you will."

"You know that I can't command their boat."

Chambers let his vessel fall astern. He had made up his mind that his voyage was doomed to bad luck. He wanted to go back to England. So he sailed away, carrying most of John Smith's belongings with him.

Whether he liked it or not, John Smith was now a pirate.

The Pirate Ship

☙ THE CAPTAIN OF THE FRENCH
privateer let John Smith wander freely about
the ship as it sailed through the empty ocean.
But the freedom to spend his days in idleness
gave John no pleasure.

With any luck, he would have been in
America by now, building his colony in
Massachusetts. He could see it all in his
mind, just as he had planned it—the wall of
the fort built of logs, the guns mounted on
platforms, four neat little houses for his men.

He had failed this year. Next year he
would try again.

He stood on deck looking over the water toward America, as he had stood once in the church tower of Willoughby. He had come a long way since those childhood days and his dreams had come a long way, too. He no longer thought adventure had to mean wars and knighthood. He smiled to remember the days when Robert and Peregrine had jokingly called him "Captain." Robert was Lord Willoughby now and Peregrine had just celebrated his wedding with festivities that had been the talk of London. But for all their titles and wealth they had had no such life as his own. And when he had escaped from these pirates and shipped again to America to found his colony, and had built his house there, it would be all of his own making.

Suddenly, he beat his fist on the rail, and threw his head back. He walked to the captain's cabin.

"Can you let me have the use of pen and paper?" he asked.

"Certainly, Captain. Sit here at my table. Take what you need."

John Smith began to write. If he could not go to America, he could write about it once more. He would tell about that northern part which he loved. He would explain how to start a colony there. He would get his map engraved and put it into the book. Then all England could read about the beautiful country he had seen. And it would be easy for him to raise the money for another voyage.

All day he worked at his book. The next day he wrote more. He began to think of a title. What would he call it? What name could he give to the country that would make it separate from Virginia?

The French, he knew, called the northern country Canada. Earlier explorers had used the name Norumbega. But John Smith wanted a good English name for a country that would some day be settled by Englishmen.

"New England!" he said to himself. He took a blank sheet of paper and wrote in large letters: A DESCRIPTION OF NEW ENGLAND. He leaned back to look at it. He nodded his head. Then he put it on top of the pages he had written.

As he took up his pen again he heard a sailor cry from the masthead: "A sail! A sail!"

A few minutes later Captain Poyrune opened the door. "I will ask you as a gentleman to stay in the cabin," he said. "I will not lock the door."

John stepped to the window which hung out over the ship's stern. A small ship came into view. As John watched, the English flag was hoisted up her mast.

Soon the French were taking away load after load of barrels and boxes. John lifted up his head and sniffed. Yes, it was cod. The ship had probably just come back from fishing off Newfoundland or New England.

At last the English ship was allowed to sail away. Captain Poyrune came to the door. "Thank you," he said.

John Smith walked out onto the deck. The ship's mate stood at the main mast with a pile of clothes beside him. He held up each piece and sold it to the highest bidder. John needed clothes badly, but he would not bid for any that had been stolen from an English ship.

Two days later four Spanish ships sailed up over the horizon from America.

"You wish to fight with us?" Captain Poyrune asked John. "The Spanish are no friends of the English—yes?"

"You will give me my share of what we take?"

"But of course, Captain."

"Then give me a sword and a pistol."

Already the sailors were charging the long row of cannons on the gun deck. As soon as the Spanish ships were close enough, the French fired a broadside. Cannon balls tore through the Spanish sails and splintered the wooden sides of the ships.

The Spanish guns answered. Soon the air was full of smoke and the sharp smell of gunpowder. Cannon balls crashed into the rigging and fell with a thud to the deck. The wounded were carried below and new men took their places. For five hours the ships exchanged shots. Neither side would give up.

"Close in on them and board them," Captain John said to Poyrune.

"But Captain, they still fire at us."

"What of that? We'll silence their guns when we get to them."

But Poyrune would not close in. At last he gave up and sailed away. But his sailors had heard what Captain Smith said.

"If we had him for a captain we would catch some rich prizes," they muttered.

Meanwhile John Smith went to Poyrune. "If you will do me the honor, I will lead a boarding party the next time we meet a Spanish ship," he said.

"With pleasure, Captain."

The next ship they met was from Brazil, a Portuguese colony. But Spain and Portugal were under one government at this time.

"There'll be pieces of eight aboard her," John told the men. "Are you ready to board her?"

"Yes! Yes!" they shouted.

The ships crashed together. Captain John jumped up onto the rail with a pistol in one hand and a sword in the other. He leaped onto the Brazilian's deck. One shot crippled the first man to attack him. There was no time to reload. Raising his sword, he rushed across the deck. A few bullets whistled past his ears. But Smith and the French sailors pushed on so fast that the Brazilians could not reload. In a few minutes the fight was over. Three hundred and seventy chests of sugar, a hundred hides, and thirty thousand pieces of eight were taken with the ship.

The privateersmen were delighted at such a big haul, and with Captain Smith for the dashing way he led them. They compared him with their own captain. Beside John Smith, Poyrune seemed weak and cowardly. Poyrune knew what the sailors were thinking. He smiled and praised Captain Smith. But he made his own plans.

Two days later, a big Spanish ship-of-war came in view, headed home from America.

"She'll be full of treasure," John told his men.

All morning, the ships fired their guns at each other. At last John Smith persuaded Poyrune to close in. Again he went over the side at the head of his men. The Spaniards fought hard, but at last they gave in. Their ship was richly loaded with treasure belonging to the King of Spain. The ship also carried many wealthy passengers, Spaniards returning home. Captain John made them line up with their belongings. They had gold and silver, rich costumes and fine jewelry.

A French crew went aboard to take the ship to France.

John Smith returned to Poyrune's ship and reported to the captain.

"A very good prize, Captain Smith," said Poyrune. "You like this work—yes?"

"I would like better to go home."

"Your share is now ten thousand crowns. Can you make so much money at home, Captain Smith?"

"I have other reasons for going home," he said.

"Aha—a fair lady, perhaps?"

John made no answer. He could not tell Poyrune he wanted to prepare another voyage to America. The French were also interested in the northern coast. Already the two nations had clashed. John knew that Captain Argall had ventured north from Jamestown and burned several French settlements.

"Well, Captain Smith, I have good news for you. We have so many prizes to take home, we will sail for France at once."

So after nearly three months on the French privateer, John Smith headed back toward Europe.

When the ships were close to the French coast, he went to Poyrune's cabin.

"Do you wish to give me my share now?" he said.

"Yes, Captain. We have a surprise for you." He called four men into the cabin. "Seize him!" he said. "He is the English captain who burned the French settlements in America. We will have him thrown in prison when we reach France."

"This fits well with the rest of your character," said John Smith. "I might have expected this from a coward. You know that it was not I, but Argall, who burned the French settlements."

Poyrune shrugged. "If you will sign a paper giving up your share in the prizes, I will not send you to prison."

"Never!" said John Smith.

That night he watched his chance. At the end of a rainstorm which had driven everyone below decks, he crept up the hatchway and into the ship's dory which was tied at the stern. He slipped the knot, let the boat drift away, and felt around for the oars. There were none in the boat!

Already a strong current was carrying him out to sea. High waves rocked the little dory. He found a pike in the bottom of the boat and tried to row with it, but he could make no headway against the rising storm.

Sheets of rain drove against him. Waves broke and sent floods of water into the boat. John cupped his hands and tried to bail out the water but it came in faster than he could get rid of it.

All night long he fought to keep his boat afloat, expecting any minute to feel it sink beneath him. When dawn came, the tide turned and swept the little craft in toward shore. John was too weak and cold to help himself. The boat nudged its way into a marsh.

There, two huntsmen found him, took him home, fed him, dried his clothes and let him sleep. He sold the boat in order to get to the port of La Rochelle. Captain Poyrune's ships should be there now. He intended to get his share of the prize.

However, neither Poyrune nor the rich Spanish prize were in the harbor. Both ships had gone down in the storm. With them had gone Poyrune and half his crew, as well as all those pieces of eight.

Again, John Smith headed for England with nothing but the clothes on his back and the water-smeared pages of his manuscript which had never left his pocket.

John Smith Explores the Future

⊞ SIX MONTHS LATER IN THE EARLY
summer of 1616, John Smith stood waiting in
a room of the King's palace at Whitehall in
London. Under his arm was a freshly printed
copy of *A Description of New England* and
his hand-drawn map. At his side stood his
old friend Robert Bertie, now Lord Willoughby and an official in the royal household.

Double doors opened at the other end of
the room. Page boys bowed. A pale but
handsome young lad of sixteen walked in. He
was Prince Charles, who would be the next

king of England.   Behind him came a crowd
of attendants.

Robert introduced John to the prince.

The bearded captain bowed low and presented his book to young Charles.   He un-
rolled his map.

"If it would please Your Highness to give
English names to this coast," he said, "I shall
have them engraved in my map."

A table was brought.   John spread out his
map and described each of the harbors and
rivers.   To each, the young prince gave a
name.

Working down the coast, he came at last
to a good harbor protected by an island.

"It is a fair spot, Your Highness, as fine as
the Plymouth harbor."

"Let it be Plymouth," said Prince Charles.
John Smith wrote the name in ink.

"Thank you, Your Highness," said Captain
John.   "And now, for the name of the whole
region, which will someday be a new
England —"

"I see you have written New England,"
said the Prince.   "Let it stand.   It has a
hopeful sound."

John Smith hurried off to the engraver's.
The map was soon printed and folded into the

copies of the book. Copies of the title page were tacked up here and there on posts in the center of London. And at the bookseller's door an apprentice stood and called to the passing crowd:

"What lack you, gentlemen? See a new book come forth, sir! Buy a new book, sir! See a new book about New England in America!"

Soon all London was talking about New England. It had a hopeful sound, as Prince Charles had said.

The new book contained the writing John had done on the pirate's ship, the engraved map with the names Prince Charles had chosen. To add to these sixty pages, Smith had asked friends of his to write some poems. Two of the poets were soldiers with whom John had fought in Hungary, one was a cousin, but at least four had known Virginia and were full of praise for the part the little captain had played in the New World.

And on the cover page Smith's name was dressed out in a new title: "John Smith: Admiral of New England."

After so much bad luck, John now had a happy stroke of fortune. Pocahontas arrived in England! Everyone knew that she was the

Indian princess who had saved Smith's life. Now everyone wanted to buy his new book.

After John Smith had left Virginia, Captain Argall had taken Pocahontas prisoner and carried her to Jamestown. There, one of the young settlers, John Rolfe, had fallen in love with her. He had married her and they had brought their little baby, Thomas, to England with them.

The news of Pocahontas' arrival reached London ahead of her. She herself would come by ship along the seacoast and up the river from Plymouth. With her was a group of ten or twelve young Indian girls and Powhatan's friend Uttamatomakkin. John Smith was concerned lest the royal court forget that Pocahontas was a princess in her own country. Dare he, a humble subject, make a suggestion to the Queen? He did write telling how Pocahontas had saved his life and how good it would be for the Virginia plantation if the Indian princess were royally received.

But for many weeks he made no move to see the girl himself, though he did see his old friend Uttamatomakkin.

"Powhatan bade me find you out," the warrior told John. "He desires that you show me your god, and also the King, Queen and

Prince you told so much about. You show me?"

Powhatan had also given Uttamatomakkin the job of counting the number of people who lived in England. "Get a long stick," Powhatan had told him. "Every time you see a new face, make a notch."

So Uttamatomakkin had come off the ship at London with his stick and knife. Within a few hours he had thrown away his notched stick. There were more people in London than he had thought there were in the whole world.

Pocahontas and her party were taken down to Brentford, a small town near London. Here she was the guest of the Bishop of London in his big, plain, three-story brick house.

She had learned to walk with small steps, to wear shoes, to manage stiff brocaded skirts, to sit indoors on high-backed chairs. Her ways had become English ways.

Of course John Smith was eager to see the girl who had saved his life, fed the colony at Jamestown, and spent so many hours with him. But he hesitated, unable to ignore the fact that she was a princess and the guest of a bishop. At last with several friends he rode down to Brentford, to the house of the Bishop.

Pocahontas entered the room on the arm of her husband. She was even more beautiful than the girl he had left seven years before. She wore a rich dress of brocaded velvet with a stiff lace collar around her neck. The garments made her big eyes look darker than ever, her gold-tinted skin even more golden.

She gave John Smith a long look out of those dark eyes, then she bowed and left the room. John had told his friends how well the Indian princess could speak English. But she had not spoken a word.

For two or three hours John Smith and John Rolfe talked about Jamestown. They talked of the fertile soil of Virginia where tobacco was now being grown at a profit.

Then Pocahontas came back into the room. She was smiling now. She held one hand at her breast, the fingers pointing toward her throat. Around her neck were the white beads John had given her.

"Do you remember these, Captain Smith?" she asked.

"I remember that you saved my life, Princess. Those poor beads were all I could give you in thanks."

"You gave me my English tongue," she said. Pocahontas walked to a window. John Smith followed her. They could speak now without being heard.

"Why did you not come sooner, my father?" Pocahontas asked. "I have waited for you."

"You are a princess, my Lady. You must not call me father."

"When you were in our country, you called my father your father. You were a stranger in our country. Now I am a stranger in yours. So you must be my father."

"I dare not let you call me that. You are a king's daughter."

"You dare not? You were not afraid of anything in our country. Why should you be afraid in your own? I tell you I will call you father, and you will call me child. They told me at Jamestown that you were dead. I thought it was true until we came to England. That is why I could not speak when I first saw you, after so many years."

"You are very kind to me, child." The word slipped out. But he was glad he had said it when he saw her smile.

"My father—will you now show me your country as I showed you mine? Can we not be together as we were then?"

John Smith shook his head. "There, I was the leader, the president. It was fit for me to deal with your father, the king, and with you. But here, I am of no importance. You will be entertained by the king himself, by all the great people of the land. But you must forget me, child."

"No, father, I will never forget you," said Pocahontas.

John Smith saw Pocahontas several times that winter. She seemed happier talking with him of the days they spent in America than when she was at the court of the English king.

Then, in March, John Rolfe prepared to take his wife and little son back to Virginia. Pocahontas boarded the *George*, bound for America, but before the ship had reached the mouth of the Thames, the young stranger so far from home had a sudden sickness. The vessel put in at Gravesend and Pocahontas was carried ashore. In just a few days, she was dead.

John Smith was in the yard of Saint Paul's Cathedral listening to the usual gossip. He heard two couriers speak the name of Pocahontas and stopped to listen: ". . . taken off the ship at Gravesend—to her end and to her grave."

With sorrow John Smith heard the news. Pocahontas had been the one soft and loving thing in his hard, soldiering life. She would always remain in his mind as the playful, laughter-loving girl of the forest.

At Plymouth, he saw the child of Pocahontas, in the arms of one of the Indian girls who had accompanied their princess to England. He had been left to grow up in the homeland of his father. John Rolfe feared to expose his son to another ocean voyage. The little dark-haired boy had eyes like Pocahontas—dark and deeply lighted. But he did not have her gay laugh that John Smith remembered with such pleasure. Poor play-loving Pocahontas . . .

*   *   *

John Smith was at Plymouth, getting three ships ready for a voyage to his beloved New England. At last he was going to have his colony! Only fifteen men would settle in his colony at first. The rest would return to England with the ships; but each year more settlers would go. In time John Smith would govern a large colony.

John Smith felt that this expedition would succeed. He knew more than any man about America. He had proven himself a brave man, able to deal with the Indians. He knew how to live in the wilderness. He knew the best route to New England. He knew where to fish, so that the merchants who paid for the voyage would make a profit.

There was only one needful thing he did not know. How could you make the wind blow?

For three months he waited with his ships in Plymouth Harbor. But the wind never came.

The whole fishing fleet of a hundred sails was delayed in Plymouth Harbor that summer. When a wind finally came, the vessels that were bound for the Newfoundland fishing banks sailed away. However, John Smith did not raise anchor. It was too late in the season for him to carry out his plans. He would have to wait another year.

Merchants and sailors began to whisper that John Smith carried bad luck with him. Hadn't one of his ships been nearly sunk in a storm? Hadn't he then been captured by pirates? Hadn't he nearly been drowned trying to escape from them? Hadn't he been sent home in disgrace from Jamestown? Hadn't bad luck always followed him? A voyage to the New World was risky enough.

It would be better to take no chances with such a man.

For three years John Smith tried to find merchants who would back another voyage. He went all over London, all over the western part of England, giving copies of his book to people who might be willing to support a colony. He had no luck.

At last he heard of a group of Englishmen who had been living in exile in Holland where they were allowed to live and worship according to their peculiar beliefs. John Smith didn't know or care much about the opinions of these "Pilgrims." However, when he learned that they were planning to carry their way of life to the New World—to plant a colony across the ocean for "conscience' sake" —he hastened to meet their agents.

The group had thought of going to the area claimed by the Dutch along the Hudson River. When that idea came to nothing, they had sent Robert Cushman and John Carver to see the Virginia Company in London. But the Merchant Adventurers were unwilling to guarantee them the privilege of worship according to their beliefs.

They read John Smith's *Description of New England* and talked with him. They studied his map and listened with interest to his proposal of making immediate profits by fishing.

Smith offered to go along as military commander to give them the protection they would need, to deal with the Indians.

"I know America well," he told them. "You will need a military man to protect you from Indian attack. I can show you where the fishing is. I can lead you to the best place to make a settlement and teach you how to set up housekeeping in the wilderness."

"We have read your book, Captain Smith," they said. Then they asked him many questions about America, both Virginia and New England.

Perhaps they, too, had heard the stories about John Smith as the bringer of bad luck. Perhaps they thought he was too strong a personality who would try to rule their colony. They had ideas of their own which they wished to carry out in the New World. Anyway, they refused to take him along. "It is cheaper to buy your books and maps than to hire you," they told him.

When they left England, they spoke as if they would settle in Virginia. But their ship, the *Mayflower*, went to New England, and they settled at the place which was already

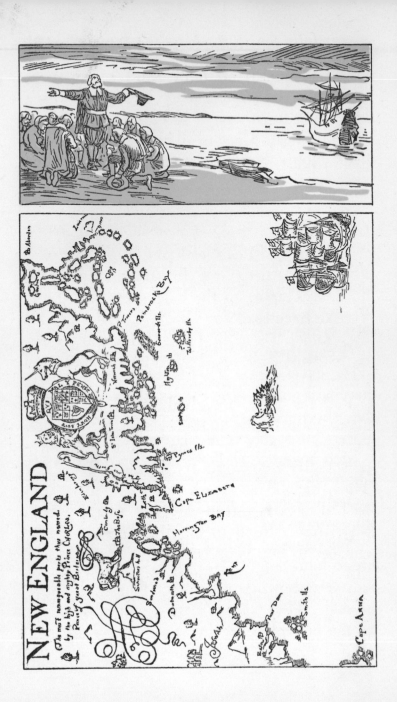

named Plymouth on John Smith's fine map.

Twenty years later, when Plymouth was a flourishing town, one of several on the Massachusetts coast, a leader of the Pilgrim colony died. John Smith's map was still in his possession.

*   *   *

The years went by, but John Smith never gave up his hope of building a colony in New England. He wrote more books. He wrote a history of Virginia and New England and put his maps in it, and the latest news of the settlements at Jamestown and Plymouth.

"I call them my children," he wrote.

He gave copies of this book to the rich merchant guilds—the bakers, the fishmongers, the shoemakers—still hoping to raise the money for a colony of his own building.

Men began to smile or duck into doorways when they saw him coming. "Here comes Captain John Smith, breathing America," they would say.

America had indeed become the breath of life to John Smith. "There every man may be master and owner of his own labor and land," he said. That was his vision. America would be the first place in the world where all men could own their land and be their own masters.

It was a truly great idea—too great for most of the men in his day to understand. It was the idea of freedom.